SEMINAR S
General E   00069083

The Church of England 1570–1640

Andrew Foster

D0658009

LONGMAN
London and New York

LONGMAN GROUP LIMITED,
Longman House, Burnt Mill, Harlow,
Essex CM20 2JE, England
and Associated Companies throughout the world.

Published in the United States of America
by Longman Inc., New York.

© Longman Group Limited 1994

First published 1994

Set in 10/11 point Baskerville (Linotron)
Produced through Longman Malaysia, TCP

ISBN 0 582 35574 5

British Library Cataloguing in Publication Data
Foster, Andrew
  Church of England, 1570–1640. – (Seminar Studies in History)
  I. Title   II. Series
  942

  ISBN 0-582-35574-5

Library of Congress Cataloging-in-Publication Data
Foster, Andrew.
  The Church of England: 1570 –1640/Andrew Foster.
    p. cm. — (Seminar studies in history)
  Includes bibliographical references (p. 126–134) and index.
  ISBN 0-582-35574-5 : £4.99
  1. Church of England—History.   2. England—Church history.
I. Title.   II. Series.
BX5070.F67   1994
283'.42'09031—dc20   93-23462
                                                       CIP

Contents

Contents

Acknowledgements

Cover: Thomas Stirry, *A Rot amongst the Bishops or a Terrible Tempest in the Sea of Canterbury*, 1641.

Note on the system of references

A bold number in round brackets (**5**) in the text refers the reader to the corresponding entry in the Bibliography section at the end of the book. A bold number in square brackets, preceded by 'doc.' [**doc. 6**], refers the reader to the corresponding item in the section of Documents, which follows the main text. Items followed by an asterisk * the first time they appear in a paragraph are explained in the Glossary.

Introduction to the series

Under the editorship of a distinguished historian, *Seminar Studies in History* cover major themes in British and European history. The authors are acknowledged experts in their field and the volumes are works of scholarship in their own right as well as providing a survey of current historical interpretations. They are constantly updated, to take account of the latest research.

Each title has a brief introduction or background to the subject, a substantial section of analysis, followed by an assessment, a documents section and a bibliography as a guide to further study. The documents enable the reader to see how historical judgements are reached and also to question and challenge them.

The material is carefully selected to give the advanced student sufficient confidence to handle different aspects of the theme as well as being enjoyable and interesting to read. In short, Seminar Studies offer clearly written, authoritative and stimulating introductions to important topics, bridging the gap between the general textbook and the specialised monograph.

Seminar Studies in History were the creation of Patrick Richardson, a gifted and original teacher who died tragically in an accident in 1979. The continuing vitality of the series is a tribute to his vision.

Roger Lockyer

The General Editor
Roger Lockyer, Emeritus Reader in History at the University of London, is the author of a number of books on Tudor and Stuart history including *Buckingham*, a political biography of George Villiers, first Duke of Buckingham, 1592–1628, and *The Early Stuarts: A Political History of England 1603–1642*. He has also written two widely used general surveys – *Tudor and Stuart Britain* and *Habsburg and Bourbon Europe*.

Preface

The aim of this short study is to provide a history of the Church of England between c. 1570 and 1640. The volume is concerned largely with questions about the long-term stability and success of the Elizabethan Settlement, the role of the Church in the state, the way in which it was staffed, the nature of the doctrines expounded in the pulpits, the impact of all this on people, and the extent to which religious issues played a part in the origins of the British Civil War. These are not the only questions which may be posed about this topic and period, nor is the thematic structure adopted for this book unproblematical. A deliberate effort has been made to expose some of the dilemmas which any historian faces in writing such a work and to highlight controversial issues. A chronological chart has been supplied, designed to facilitate alternative 'readings' of events through different columns, and to prompt thoughts of how 'facts' shift focus according to different perspectives.

It is important to remember that we never come 'cold' to any historical period or problem. Our views are always subtly conditioned by approaches adopted in the past, the nature and range of historical evidence employed, and the relevance of what we are studying to the times in which we live – which in turn determine the questions we now ask. Certain traditions and concepts have dominated all past approaches to this topic, and the views of some prominent commentators have been included amongst the documents to set this larger historiographical scene. The controversies of the seventeenth century have long tentacles. Hence, one traditional way of viewing this period stems from Peter Heylyn, chaplain to Archbishop William Laud, who naturally viewed his master kindly and firmly blamed Puritans for causing the Civil War. For William Prynne, on the other hand, who had himself suffered for attacks on ecclesiastical policy in the 1630s, the war was brought about by Arminians and crypto-Papists. The contrast between these two views is starkly exposed in their different accounts of the career of the prominent Arminian, Archbishop Richard Neile [**docs 1** and **2**].

Thanks largely to the work of Whig historians such as Thomas B. Macaulay and Samuel R. Gardiner in the nineteenth century, when great emphasis was placed on Parliament and England's constitutional progress, the tradition which stressed the role of Puritans became dominant, although they were now presented in a sympathetic light [**doc. 3**] This was also a reflection of the well-known phenomenon that winners get most attention in history. The stress on Puritanism lasted well into the twentieth century, when Christopher Hill demonstrated how easily Gardiner's concept of a 'Puritan Revolution' could be incorporated within a broadly Marxist framework. Puritanism, as he defined it, became the religion of the 'industrious sort of people', and his incredible range of books have always reminded us of the importance of seeing religious affairs in a social as well as a political context [**doc. 4**] (**69–74**).

More recently, as our own times have become more unsettled, so we have been provided with a sudden plethora of alternative inter-pretations of this period. Close analysis of the complex points of theology which interested those decried by Puritans as 'Arminians' led Nicholas Tyacke to appreciate virtues in the case once outlined so strenuously by William Prynne, and to argue that 'religion became an issue in the Civil War crisis due primarily to the rise to power of Arminianism in the 1620s' (**192**, p. 119). No sooner had this view become established, however, than it too was assailed on all sides by others who wished to place emphasis on the actions of the King, stress short-term causes of the war, and prefer to do without the concept of Arminianism. At least the Royalist cause is now gaining close scrutiny (**54, 110, 126, 128, 185, 194**).

As controversy sparks again over issues once deemed dead, other voices rightly urge us to avoid seeing all things according to a simplistic polarity between Puritans and Arminians (**64, 83, 84**). Moderates like Joseph Hall and Thomas Fuller demand attention, while the views of the majority of ordinary people in the parishes remain largely hidden from view. To some extent, this reflects general problems which stem from the nature and range of sources which have affected study of these issues. Most attention has been devoted in the past to central records, state papers, and the records of diocesan administration. It has always been easier to approach this topic from the 'top down', given a convenient supply of letter collections and biographies of bishops and statesmen of this period. It is only slowly that historians are finding ways of offsetting material from the institutional, formal, official sources, against the more obviously partisan accounts of Prynne and Heylyn, whilst also keeping the local perspective of ordinary people in focus. The process of re-selection and re-focusing continues and should always be challenged. In the choice of primary material for this book, an attempt has been made to cover sources from as wide a range as possible, and to indicate where the interpretation of certain documents lies at the heart of current controversies.

It is hoped that by adopting a thematic structure, certain issues can be made to stand out more clearly for the reader. Analysis of the chapter headings used in the creation of this text is in itself revealing. Use of the term 'Elizabethan Legacy' at the outset carries with it a number of assumptions and ideas to be reviewed later. The decision to provide chapters on the episcopate, the clerical profession, and Church and people reflects a modern, rather 'functionalist' approach to these matters. A chapter on the Church in the 1630s reflects the current feeling that this decade is worthy of close study and may provide the key to understanding why war broke out in 1642 (**50, 54, 110, 150**). Yet that should not distract the reader from noting that many important themes in the history of the Church turn on an interpretation of the significance of events in the 1590s, 1603, and 1625.

Many people have influenced the construction of this book and deserve special thanks: my good friends and colleagues, Keith Jenkins, Clive Behagg, Patrick Preston, Ray Verrier, and John Fines, who have contributed much to my understanding of the nature of history and how it might be taught; John made typically terse and apposite comments on this work in draft. Kenneth Fincham also kindly read and commented extensively on earlier drafts, giving me the benefit of his impressive knowledge of the early Stuart Church. Christopher Hill started me off on these enquiries many years ago, but it would be difficult to name the many friends who have sustained me since; including students of my Special Subject group, sixth-formers and their teachers. Annabel Jones has shown great patience while she waited on Longman's behalf for this text; Roger Lockyer has been a model editor: painstaking, clear, and firm while encouraging. Finally, there is my wife, Liz, to whom I dedicate this book with love and thanks.

Andrew Foster,
West Sussex Institute

Part One: The Background

1   An 'Elizabethan Church Legacy'?

The use of all historical concepts entails simplification and distortion, but the concept of an 'Elizabethan Church legacy' has value and a long pedigree (**68**). In a sermon preached before members of Parliament in 1643, Thomas Fuller informed his congregation that Queen Elizabeth had 'swept the Church of England, and left all the dust behind the door' (**17**, p. 142). Nineteenth-century historians acknowledged that Elizabeth left unresolved problems, yet attached greater blame to James I and Charles I for handling their inheritance badly. Now the pendulum has swung again and historians are being more critical of Elizabeth (**61, 64, 66, 91**). Discussion of a 'legacy' focuses the mind on the state of religious affairs at a critical juncture in 1603, provokes analysis of important trends, and highlights themes deemed central to this book. It is wise to remember, however, that this approach may distort our sense of period, exaggerate the importance of 1603 as a 'turning point', and should be set against a 'Jacobean legacy' in 1625.

Any discussion of the history of the Church of England should start with consideration of the fragile compromise on which it was based in 1559. Historians now regard the Acts of Supremacy and Uniformity, which established the nature of the Church, as a hard-won compromise extracted by the Queen in the face of considerable pressure from conservative Catholic forces and Protestant extremists (**63, 80**). The Thirty-nine Articles of 1562–63 completed the makeshift settlement by providing the Church with a set of canons* governing its doctrine. These were only reluctantly ratified by Parliament in 1571, anxious to maintain its role in the making of this religious settlement. Yet it would be wise to remember that for many in those early years of the reign, this settlement was seen as merely the beginning of a Protestant reformation and not a final solution. Many of the returning Protestant exiles who took key positions in this Church did so very reluctantly, and had strong misgivings, particularly over the retention of episcopacy* and the apparatus of the old Church courts. Puritan patrons like the Earl of Leicester found themselves criticised when they dared to support bishops [**doc. 6**].

A Puritan threat to stability?

A body of clergy and laity swiftly emerged within the Elizabethan Church to whom the label 'Puritan'* became attached because of their particular piety and concern for 'further reformation'. It was a term of abuse which gathered more connotations, mostly seen as subversive, as the period in question progressed. These shifts in usage over time have led many historians to question the value of the concept of 'Puritanism', but the general consensus remains that this term had meaning for contemporaries and still has its uses today. They were 'the hotter sort of Protestants'. Early disputes centred on the use of clerical vestments* ('rags of Rome'), and the nature of Church services. Archbishop Parker was tough with dissidents, but the issues re-surfaced in the Millenary Petition of 1603 [**doc. 5**] (**39, 45, 48, 52, 55, 57, 71, 78, 83, 84, 151, 159**).

Puritans valued the Bible highly, and so worried greatly about the need for an educated ministry to preach the word. The late sixteenth century was marked by a tremendous expansion in the number of schools and university colleges, the like of which was not seen again in this country until the twentieth century. This was a tribute to the success of Protestantism with the ruling elite and was one way in which reformation was to be propagated. It did, however, create tensions when an increasingly educated laity noted weaknesses in the standards of their clergy. Attempts were made to remedy abuses – for example, in Canons* promulgated in 1576, and orders put before Convocation* in 1589 [**doc. 18**]. Gradually, thanks to the expansion of Oxford and Cambridge, the situation improved. The Queen and her archbishops were ambivalent about clerical self-help initiatives, such as 'exercises'* and 'prophesyings'*, and suppressed them as potentially subversive. Puritan surveys critical of clerical standards were a feature of the 1580s, and the tactic was repeated in 1603 prior to the Hampton Court Conference*.

Clashes with bishops in the Church hierarchy drove some intellectuals like Thomas Cartwright and William Travers into espousing Presbyterian beliefs concerning the best form of Church organisation (**61**). Presbyterianism* was based on Calvin's Geneva, and employed pastors, teachers, elders, and deacons. A growing disenchantment with bishops can be charted from the Admonition controversy* of the early 1570s, through the writings of Thomas Wood, to the notorious *Martin Marprelate* tracts of the 1580s. Although many dallied with Presbyterian ideas in the 1570s and 80s, the war with Spain brought about the greater sense of Protestant unity sought by the authorities. Clerical subscription to three articles pertaining to the essential tenets of the Church of England – namely, belief in the royal supremacy, the Canons* and the prescribed liturgy* (the last two of which had aroused controversy in 1571) was more forcefully required by Whitgift after 1583 [**doc. 7**]. The device was enshrined in the Canons of 1604 and became the prime instrument used to secure uniformity amongst the clergy. Although there were those who 'separated' – whether as Brownists* or as Presbyterians* – the word 'Puritan' was applied to those who remained *within* the Church of England, and in 1603, at James I's accession, they were still an influential group.

At the root of many Puritan concerns for the Church lay doubts about its continued 'Catholic' traditions – that is, aspects of Church government like the retention of bishops and deans; the use of clerical vestments*; continued use of ceremonies like that of the sign of the cross in baptism; and the persistence of an apparatus of Church courts still operating within a system of canon law. All found expression in the clauses of the Millenary Petition [**doc. 5**]. And such doubts and fears were constantly fanned during this period by the continued presence of Catholic recusants* in England – those who refused to attend the Church of England. The activities of Catholic missionaries increased dramatically after 1568 with the establishment of an English seminary at Douai. The influx of Jesuits* after 1580 raised more anxieties, for they were seen as instruments of the devil who plotted the death of the Queen (**40, 41, 56, 129, 156**).

The strength of Puritanism* as a strictly clerical movement had faded by 1603, so much so that some historians used to talk of a late Elizabethan calm. Yet Puritanism was potentially far more subversive in so far as it had become a 'social ethic'. Concern over vestments* and ceremonies remained, but issues like Sabbatarianism*, preaching and a godly lifestyle were now uppermost in the minds of a significant number of people and were used as a way of judging all things, including the royal Court. It is on these matters that Christopher Hill has made such a valuable contribution to our understanding of the concept of Puritanism, and upon which Lucy Hutchinson provides such strong testimony [**doc. 12**] (**71, 72**).

A Catholic threat to stability?

It is vital to remember at all times the effect of the presence of Catholics in England upon Protestants. The crescendos of complaints – closely linked with the passage of legislation against Catholics in Parliament – usually ebbed and flowed in tune with foreign policy; hence new laws in the 1580s and later Bills when England was at war in the 1620s. The feeling of being in a permanent battle against the Papal Antichrist was a powerful one and a hallmark of Puritanism* (**72, 78, 84, 195**). Yet there were paradoxes in the treatment of English Catholics. In one sense they represented a dangerous, sizeable minority – approximately 750,000 to 1 million people – including about about one-fifth of the aristocracy. Yet there was also a growing awareness amongst the ruling elite that these people were not really a major threat to the stability of the state. In the localities Protestant gentry happily continued to rub shoulders with their Catholic counterparts. In some regions, notably the north, Catholic gentry held important offices in local government well into the seventeenth century (**59**).

As splits emerged in the Catholic missionary ranks, Robert Cecil took advantage of the 'Wisbech stirs'* and later Appellant controversy* to encourage talk of Catholics taking a limited form of Oath of Allegiance (**137**). Secular priests*, angered by the imperialistic designs of the Jesuits*, toyed with this idea. The Gunpowder Plot of 1605, which was once interpreted as evidence that Catholic unrest was an important ingredient of the Elizabethan legacy, is now regarded as marking a distinct end to one phase of the history of Catholics in England (**129**). The peace which Cecil negotiated with Spain in 1604 was much more significant, and a much more apt comment on the way events had been moving over the last years of Elizabeth's reign. Under the Stuarts, Catholic families like the Howards returned to court favour, and the fortunes of Catholics in general improved steadily over the seventeenth century.

Economic problems of the Church

The Protestant Reformation in England was associated with the removal of a vast amount of property from the hands of the Church. Elizabeth's reign only served to facilitate further asset-stripping and to weaken the economic foundations of the new Church of England. Under Henry VIII, six new dioceses had been formed, of which five survived, but they were all poorly endowed. Under the Act of Exchanges of 1559, Elizabeth gave herself the right to exchange property with her bishops, usually to their disadvantage. Worse still, in several notorious cases, she left dioceses without bishops for many years: Bristol for fourteen years, Ely for nineteen and Oxford for forty-one. Many of her favourites, particularly Leicester, were given Church offices as sinecures or benefited from gifts of Church property (**66, 70**). In *A Treatise of Ecclesiasticall Discipline* published in 1590, Matthew Sutcliffe lamented that those who had 'devoured the late lands of Abbeys, their stomachs are now so eager that they can digest not only tithes, but also glebe* and parish churches' (**37,** p.2, Epistle).

The late sixteenth century witnessed a period of sustained inflation which hurt all those on fixed incomes. The Crown had recourse to the sale of land and crafty exploitation of the Church; the latter had few resources at its disposal. One result of the Reformation had been that almost half the better livings in England and Wales had passed into the hands of lay impropriators* (according to the contemporary historian Sir Henry Spelman, 3,849 out of 9,244), invariably providing them with the great tithes*, and thus the major part of any income attached to the living. Only one-third of all parishes were deemed capable of providing an adequate stipend at this period. To the embarrassment of many bishops, they were forced to exchange land for impropriations*, thus making them too part and parcel of a vicious circle (**70**).

Christopher Hill's bleak picture of this 'plunder of the church' has been softened by the work of Claire Cross and Felicity Heal (**52, 65, 66, 70**). Not all dioceses suffered badly and not all bishops saw a major reduction in their income, even if the sources of that income were changed in nature from land to spiritualities* (namely, impropriations*). In effect, as Hill pointed out, the bishops were still rich and powerful enough to be envied, but during the reign of Elizabeth their power base had been significantly eroded. Moreover, the source of much of their income brought bishops into conflict with the interests of their own clergy and rendered reform difficult, as was found at the very outset of James I's reign, when he idealistically suggested that the Crown, universities, and bishops should set an example by restoring Church property to the clergy. He was quickly warned of how much he stood to lose by that suggestion, and subsequently backed down.

Ordinary clergymen generally fared badly; hence the need for practices like the holding of several livings in 'plurality' resulting in 'non-residence', much despised by Puritans. Yet once again, a largely gloomy picture has been modified by recent research (**65**). Clergymen in town livings tended to suffer most, owing to loss of glebe* land and the difficulty of calculating and collecting tithes*, not to mention the poor salaries usually attached to such livings. Rectors* of rural parishes were in the best position: they not only retained their great tithes (those payable on large animals and crops), but also usually had access to reasonable glebe land which they could farm or lease for profit. Godly Puritans compensated for the poverty of urban livings by establishing lectureships* and market-day sermons to supplement the income of local clergy. This was one reason why towns became beacons of light for some, and centres of sedition in the eyes of others. Lay patronage of livings and lectureships raised perennial problems about who controlled the Church. These were to culminate in the 1630s with Archbishop Laud's attacks on the Feoffees for Impropriations*, a group which patronised Puritan ministers (**66, 106, 130**).

There are thus several ways in which the economic problems of the Church were significant in this period. There was a slight erosion in the power and prestige of bishops owing to decreasing economic muscle; poor livings meant that it was difficult to attract educated clergy to some parts of the country; the sources of revenue could bring clergy into conflict with clergy, but more frequently clergy into conflict with laity, particularly over the issue of tithes*. It is possible that these problems distracted some bishops from their spiritual concerns, and certainly bishops of the seventeenth century were required to think about diocesan estate management in ways not dreamed of in the years before 1600.

Most interestingly, this is one area in which James I has traditionally had a good press. One of his first actions on becoming King was to bring in an Act against diminution of possessions of archbishops and bishops and for avoiding dilapidations* (1604). This halted spoliation of the Church by the Crown, and Christopher Hill noted the irony that 'The parsimonious Elizabeth was supreme plunderer of the church; the extravagant James was defender of its revenues (**70**, p. 32). James seems to have appreciated more than Elizabeth that attacks on bishops might eventually lead to attacks on the Crown; hence his celebrated comment: 'No Bishop, No King' (**70,** p. 33).

The royal supremacy

This topic is discussed at greater length below (pp. 13–22), but it is an important ingredient in any debate about an 'Elizabethan legacy' because here is a classic arena in which Elizabeth is deemed to have done well in contrast with the Stuarts. The crucial point is that the English Reformation was accomplished as an act of state by Crown and Parliament. This was not only true of the reforms of Henry VIII and Edward VI, but even of Mary, who had no choice but to use Parliament when she sought to reverse matters. Later, of course, Parliament was vital in the proceedings of 1559 (**80**). Needless to say, this produced great tensions. Religion was a matter on which members of Parliament, most particularly the House of Commons, felt they had a duty as well as a right to speak their minds. Elizabeth, for her part, felt that as Supreme Governor of the Church of England, once the settlement had been made, control of religious policy was a matter for her alone. Puritan 'Admonitions'* to Parliament in 1572 called for better ministers, plainer worship, and greater ecclesiastical discipline to be obtained through a simplified Church structure. Virtually every Parliament witnessed an attempt to introduce legislation concerning some aspect of Church government or liturgy, the most heated debates coming in 1586 and 1587 when moves were made to change the Prayer Book (**45**).

In theory, the Queen was correct in claiming full rights to act as Supreme Governor and her position was buttressed by the writings first of Bishop Jewel in his *Apology*, directed chiefly at Catholics, and later of Richard Hooker in his *Laws of Ecclesiastical Polity* (**11**). Elizabeth played the role of 'nursing mother' to her church and constantly employed all her arts of propaganda to that effect. In practice, too, Elizabeth played a leading part: it was Elizabeth who prompted Archbishop Parker to stand firm over vestments*; it was she who discouraged clerical marriages. The most celebrated example of the exercise of her power came with her sequestration* of Archbishop Grindal in 1577, when he rejected her orders to outlaw the holding of prophesyings* or exercises* carried out by the godly to raise clerical standards. Grindal remained suspended from his full duties for the rest of his life and was lucky not to be dismissed completely (**46**).

Even towards the end of her long reign, Elizabeth kept control over her church. When Archbishop Whitgift, possibly the archbishop she felt closest to, and certainly the only one to whom she

ever gave a seat on her Privy Council, issued the Lambeth Articles*
in 1595 in an effort to stop controversies at Cambridge over
doctrine, Elizabeth ordered them to be withdrawn [**doc. 16**]. It
could be argued that acceptance of the Lambeth Articles might at
least have codified religious doctrine on predestination* and given
the Church respite from problems to come, but Elizabeth was the
mistress of the ambiguous gesture and comment, and may have
had surer instincts than her 'little black husband' in ducking this
particular theological problem.

James I has been criticised because he raised Puritan hopes, first
by accepting the Millenary Petition in 1603, and then by holding
the Hampton Court Conference* in 1604 [**docs 5** and **29**]. Yet this
was simply his way of demonstrating who was Supreme Governor.
He took a close interest in Church affairs and was not about to let
members of Parliament get away with any more than they had
under Elizabeth. Indeed, the hopes of Puritans were quickly
dispelled when the Convocation* of 1604 passed 141 Canons* for
the Church with scant reference to debates in Parliament [**docs 7**
and **20**]. These Canons stand as an important landmark in the
history of the Church, yet they were never formally submitted to
Parliament for approval. It was to be a similar story when Laud
presented seventeen new Canons for ratification by Convocation
in 1640 [**doc. 26**].

Under James I, the clergy began to regain some of their
confidence and lost independence, and the rift between their
interests and those of lay members of Parliament widened. The
Reformation had entailed a drastic reduction in the number of
clergymen eligible to sit in the House of Lords, and the bishops
who remained were tolerated rather than popular. Carp and criti-
cise as they might, members of Parliament saw control of the
Church slip away from their grasp to the Court and Convocation*.
The latter met concurrently with any Parliament and was
composed of clergymen. The Elizabethan tradition of energetic
debates on religious affairs continued, particularly when
discussing legislation on morals or recusants*, but Parliament
under the Stuarts acted as a sounding board for criticism and was
never really embraced as a full partner in any new initiatives.

Ironically of course, by 1603 the laity had gained control of a vast
number of Church livings through impropriations* and advowsons*, which entailed the right to present ministers for posts.
Crown and bishops might reign supreme when it came to legislation, but matters on the ground stood very differently. Thanks to

Puritanism*, the laity made increasing claims about what they wanted from the clergy, particularly in the way of preaching. Separatists took the logical step of leaving the Church to set up their own 'congregations', and so demonstrated that for some, even the supreme authority of the minister was no more. The notion of the 'priesthood of all believers' was central to the Protestant Reformation, and the shift from 'priest/magician' to 'minister/preacher' inevitably struck at the power of the clergy. Clergymen were caught in a double bind. On the one hand, able ministers would be valued highly by their godly communities; on the other, less satisfactory ministers, particularly those who came into conflict with the laity over Church rights or money, might find themselves the objects of criticism and abuse. Such attacks could come from the indifferent and wordly in the lay community, just as much as from the godly, and in general it seems the life of a minister was an increasingly exacting one during the late Elizabethan and early Stuart period.

Institutional success of the Church of England?

Whilst it is possible to point to elements of anti-clericalism in the sixteenth century, it is also important to note a partly related phenomenon of increasing clericalism. That is to say that the very success of the Church of England in this period may have brought about problems for later. As the Elizabethan Settlement survived, so it gained more outspoken defenders. The modesty and humility of the first band of bishops gave way to a more truculent attitude in the likes of Whitgift, Aylmer, and Bancroft. By the 1590s there were senior clergy in the Church who felt proud of having been 'born' into the Church of England. The institution was solidifying. Bishops like Bancroft felt able to speak out in defence of the divine origins of episcopacy*; others sought occasions to attack Puritans, whether over vestments* and ceremonies, or the vaunted status of preaching in relation to other aspects of worship. There was a new-found confidence abroad in the minds of many clergy.

Rosemary O'Day has gone so far as to argue that this period witnessed the emergence of a 'clerical profession', thanks largely to the increased number of graduates who eventually entered the ministry (**100**). It is difficult to gauge how this might have affected clerical attitudes, but it is possible that some may have felt alienated from, and less able to communicate with, their flocks. Some of the anti-clericalism which surfaced in the seventeenth century may have been fuelled by anti-intellectualism, as much as by any perceived failings in the clergy. On the other hand, a common educational background may be a strong factor in explaining why there was a revival of strident clericalism in this period, as clergy at all levels attempted to regain some of the status lost to them at the Reformation. The clergy in the Church in 1603 were very different from those who had joined Elizabeth in 1559.

New theological trends?

Coupled with the changes noted above, some clergy in the 1590s started to question tenets of the Church of England long held dear. The most notable disputes centred on the doctrine of predestination*, but this was only one issue on which 'anti-Calvinists' found scope to disagree with orthodox opinion. The supremacy of preaching was attacked, and Sabbatarianism* aroused heated debate. The theologian who sealed the institution-alisation of the Church of England, and in some measure presaged many of these theological speculations, was Richard Hooker (**84**). It was Hooker who gave the Church of England its intellectual justification; it was he who fully ratified the peculiar mixture of Catholic and Protestant practice that made up the Settlement and declared that it was intrinsically sound in its own right. It was Hooker's concept of *adiaphora*, or 'things indifferent', which freed and galvanised theologians like Lancelot Andrewes, Samuel Harsnett, and John Overall to justify ceremonial anew, to study the Fathers*, and to respect aspects of the Catholic Church without shame (**84, 98, 101, 114, 117, 118**).

Older formulation of arguments for an 'Elizabethan legacy' usually placed the threats to stability either with the Catholics, the Puritans, or the economic problems of the Church. Employing this concept today, many historians feel happier identifying the real threat to the Church as coming from these new theological ideas, especially as they were promoted by a much revitalised clergy. For Nicholas Tyacke, it was not Puritans who placed the Calvinist consensus under strain in the 1590s, but these new theologians soon to go by the name of Arminians*. His story is not about a Puritan revolution, but an Arminian counter-revolution (**118, 191**). This is a far cry from writers who once depicted this period largely in terms of a slow shift of power from the clergy to the laity, part of an inevitable process in the secularisation of society. Yet it would be wrong to over-dramatise these trends in 1603. The questioning of Calvinist orthodoxy was largely confined to select circles of theologians at Cambridge; it was not until the 1620s that they surfaced in a wider political arena (**83, 84, 101**). It is significant, however, that whereas Elizabeth had always held aloof from religious factions, James I could not resist the temptation to play the theologian and was soon drawn into the increasingly complex Church wrangles which ensued in his reign.

In all this talk of the state of the Church which James I inherited in 1603, one should not forget the enthusiasts, the missionaries of both Catholic and Protestant hue who saw themselves as fighting a lonely battle for lives and souls in an ungodly world. That battle had progressed since 1559, but it was still far from won, and the sense of struggle was a vital force in the lives of minorities in the state in and after 1603. Yet it was significant that the succession of James I was peaceful, the first since the Reformation not to herald an immediate volte-face on matters of religion. The real tensions in society in 1603 were between the religious enthusiasts and the rest, with the rest facing constant pressure from both the authorities and their parish communities (**47, 49**). This was the continuing battle to ensure that England did indeed become a godly, Protestant nation. The pace and success of the Protestant Reformation may not now seem as assured as some historians once held, but that debate will run and run (**61**). What James I inherited in 1603 was far from being a completely Protestant nation, but it was much closer to that situation than it had been in 1559. Moreover, the seeds of future problems lay not with old Protestant/Catholic rivalries, but within the nature of the newly, and now securely, established Church of England.

Part Two: Analysis

2   The Crown and the Church of England

In theory, the holder of the Crown was Supreme Governor of the Church of England, responsible, with the aid of both Parliament and Convocation*, for the doctrine and organisation of the Church. It was through the Crown that all bishops and deans were appointed, not to mention lesser officials within the Church hierarchy. Dispensations also came from the Crown, as for example when the layman Adam Newton was allowed to become Dean of Durham in 1606. The Crown was the ultimate head of all the Church courts, the highest of which was the prerogative court of High Commission (Causes Ecclesiastical)*.

In return for exercising these responsibilities, the Crown took 'first fruits* and tenths' on all livings above a certain value (in effect, a tax payment calculated on the value of the living), and also took fees during any vacancies. The Crown was also entitled to taxation in the form of clerical subsidies, voted by Convocation* at the same time as Parliament. In practice, the Crown was also the largest single holder of impropriations* and advowsons* in England and Wales, holding the right of presentation to all livings worth more than £20 per annum. Probably one-third of all the livings which fell vacant in any year lay in the gift of the Crown. Such patronage was exercised through the office of the Lord Chancellor or Lord Keeper of the Great Seal, yet there seems to have been no distinct pattern to the many appointments made through these channels (**100**). Lord Keepers like Hatton, Bacon, Williams and Coventry were advised by knowledgeable chaplains, but were subject, like everybody else at Court, to suits from interested parties. As long as the ministers proposed were learned and worthy, their choice rested on the whim of the moment or on previous promises and obligations. The system during this period was neither more corrupt and inefficient, nor any more regulated, than it had ever been (**100**).

Many practical tensions beset and disturbed this theoretical model of the royal supremacy. There were distinct ambiguities about the role of the laity (**11**). The educated elite could make reasonable claims about their rights to voice opinions on religious matters in Parliament. Godly Puritans, leading the battle for further reformation in many towns and parishes, were not readily subservient to the wishes of the Crown or bishops. There was fairly constant pressure from the laity for a greater say in the running of the Church, but this theme has possibly been over-stressed in the past. Crown rights were relatively well defended and maintained under Elizabeth and James I, and the major inroads made later owed as much to the incompetence of Charles I as to any irresistible forces at work in society. Much has been written of the subversive potential of Protestantism. As long as monarchs performed their role as 'godly princes' they were safe, but if they were seen to falter, then 'resistance theories', dormant in the writings even of loyal propagandists like John Foxe, could be activated.

Lay concerns were frequently voiced in Parliament, and this period witnessed a steady stream of Bills to do with religion. The House of Commons stoutly maintained freedom of speech over religious affairs, but could not prevent the Crown from employing Convocation* as the main agent for reform in matters of Church government and doctrine. The Canons* of 1604 were never ratified formally by Parliament; nor were the even more controversial Laudian Canons of 1640. Parliaments could thus become rather bad-tempered over religious matters, and although Bills concerning recusancy were fairly commonplace, other Bills dealing with scandalous ministers or the operation of Church courts could be guaranteed to offend the bishops. The latter felt that ecclesiastical affairs were best left in the hands of Convocation. Needless to say, bishops were often unpopular with members of the Commons, most notably (before 1640) in 1610, 1614, 1621, and 1629 (**14, 31, 104**).

Ambiguities in theory and practice were well exploited by Puritan critics over the period. As members of the establishment developed exalted notions of the divine right of bishops – beginning with Richard Bancroft's sermon at St Paul's Cross in 1589 – so Puritan critics questioned whether this doctrine tended to derogate from the authority of the Crown. What would happen, they asked, if the bishops and the Crown disagreed? In fact, such was the rapport between the first two Stuarts and their bishops that this never presented itself as a real problem. In 1629 William Prynne tried hard to exploit remarks made by the Arminian* John Cosin which appeared to slight royal authority, but all to no avail.

Charles I was no Elizabeth about to call his clergy into line; under him the clergy seem to have found a true 'partnership'. It was a galling situation for many of the laity, who feared a revival of clerical power. William Prynne stuck to his guns and questioned the legitimacy of episcopal visitations* called without direct orders from the Crown, only to be put in the pillory for his pains (**114, 118**).

Royal supremacy in practice

Enough has been said to show that Elizabeth took her role as Supreme Governor very seriously. She was a strong monarch who never allowed her bishops much freedom of action; she was always prepared to interfere, and not even Whitgift could feel safe from her scolding tongue. Yet, while she presided over the growing stability of her religious 'settlement', Elizabeth can be seen to have posed problems for her successors by her attitude towards the economic state of the Church. She may have allowed the Church to be all things to all men, but she also used it for her own advantage, and that of selected favourites. Moreover, when faced with a choice between political and pastoral imperatives, such as that posed by the decision to suppress exercises,* Elizabeth always opted for political security. As far as she was concerned, the English Reformation had been achieved and was now simply a matter of obedience as urged in the homilies* (**11, 52**).

The Jacobean *via media**

Much changed with James I. And here major shifts in viewpoint have appeared in recent years. Where once James I was regarded as merely 'the wisest fool in Christendom', a king who dabbled in ecclesiastical matters without real insight or application, he is now seen as the architect of his own *via media* (**146**). James appreciated that the Elizabethan Settlement needed some fine tuning and he initiated a number of reform measures, not least of which was the publication of the King James Authorised Version of the Bible in 1611. He did indeed believe in the Divine Right of Kings, but this was not untypical of monarchs of his day; Elizabeth probably believed much the same without feeling the need to say so. Statements about divine right did not give the offence that Whig historians once supposed (**90**). What aroused greater hostility, in the longer term, was the fact that James's reign saw an elevation in the status of the clergy and a more prominent role in government for bishops. James liked the company of clerics – not only those who stimulated his intellect, but also those who simply made him laugh. Thus we find him keeping company with the scholarly Lancelot Andrewes, the worldly Thomas Bilson, the aristocratic James Montagu, and the down-to-earth Richard Neile. Seven bishops eventually served on his Privy Council, and the urbane Bishop Williams of Lincoln even became his Lord Keeper in 1621. James stopped the asset-stripping of the Church which had been such a feature of Elizabeth's reign. He had a shrewd appreciation of the value of the Church as a prop to his own crown; he defended clerical rights and did not stoop to leaving dioceses vacant for short-term gain.

James I intervened in Church matters even more than Elizabeth, and much more openly. At the very outset of his reign, when the bishops were in turmoil at the mere suggestion, James decided to hold the Hampton Court Conference* and allow Puritans to speak their minds. The conference turned out to be a strange event, and the most radical Puritans were not present. Historians have long debated its significance, and the consensus now appears to be that it was a constructive round-table conference, even if it did reveal new divisions within the Church. The conference may not have been a wild success, but older views that it was the start of a series of errors on James's part, and simply acted to raise and then dash Puritan hopes, have been shown to be exaggerated. James used the conference to establish a policy of *via media** whereby all but the most extreme of Catholics as well as Puritans were encouraged to subscribe to his broad Church. To this end, James gave Bancroft authority to compel subscription to the Three Articles after 1604 [**doc. 7**]. And he seems to have supervised the campaigns which followed against nonconforming clergy more closely than hitherto supposed (**58, 118, 134, 135, 139, 144, 180, 188**).

By the same token, the appointment of George Abbot as Archbishop of Canterbury in 1611 is not now seen as a terrible mistake, but rather as an attempt to go for a 'Grindalian' *via media** (**124, 145, 161**). On the death of Bancroft many expected James to appoint Lancelot Andrewes as Archbishop, but the King seems to have shown a shrewd awareness of the latter's weaknesses. Andrewes was an intellectual, shy of public authority and not a great administrator; he was also associated too firmly with the minority wing of the Church who were becoming known for their 'high-church' views on ceremonial and worship – the group that were subsequently known as Arminians* (**125**). A *via media* required somebody closer to the Puritans, but somebody who would, at the same time, make a sound administrator. George Abbot seemed to be just the man, for his strong anti-Catholic credentials and recent loyal service to the King over religious affairs in Scotland showed him to be in tune with both public opinion and royal policy.

Where Elizabeth had kept her counsel on matters of theology, James revelled in debate. It is a moot point as to which was the wisest policy. The King may have developed a closer under-standing of ecclesiastical problems, but his willingness to get involved made him a clearer prey for Court factions. One fairly innocuous strand of the King's writings was related to propaganda against Catholics, chiefly over the Oath of Allegiance*. Between 1608 and 1615, and with considerable help from a team of clerics led by Montagu, Andrewes, and Barlow, James wrote the *Apology, Premonition* and *A Remonstrance* against Cardinals Bellarmine and du Perron. Robert Cecil fretted that James's literary interests distracted him from more important business, but they may have improved the King's position in the eyes of his subjects by confirming his Protestant, anti-papal stance.

The King's interest in theology did, however, embroil him in Protestant controversies. Disputes in the Netherlands about the appointment of Conrad Vorstius to the chair left vacant by the death of Arminius at Leyden University in 1609 surfaced in England in 1611. George Abbot and others sided with Dutch Calvinist friends against Vorstius, blackened his character with James I, and thus used the debate to score points against suspected Arminians* in the English Church (**187**). Here was clear evidence of religious faction-fighting at the Jacobean Court. Yet, alienated though he was by Dutch Arminianism with its taint of republi-canism, James was still shrewd enough to distinguish between home and foreign policy, and indeed to appreciate the need for different approaches to England, Scotland, and Ireland. Sound Calvinists were eventually sent as delegates to the Synod of Dort* in 1618 (see pp. 38–41), but prominent English Arminians like Overall and Andrewes were promoted to good bishoprics at home. Presbyterian* Scotland was slowly being brought into conformity with practices in England, hence the consecration of Scottish bishops in 1610 and the later Articles of Perth of 1618*. In predominantly Catholic Ireland, on the other hand, Calvinists were rewarded for their missionary efforts with a new set of

Canons* in 1615 which incorporated the controversial Lambeth Articles*.

It would be dangerous to over-emphasise the conscious, rational elements in any new understanding of this Jacobean religious strategy. The man who was once labelled a 'Bad King' because he 'slobbered at the mouth and had favourites', cannot be totally rehabilitated by modern historians (**108**, p. 69)! He did have favourites and this did distort policies occasionally. Indeed, the promotion of Arminians* in the Church owed not a little to the fact that Richard Neile was one of the King's many lesser favourites, before Laud was given the task of 'capturing' Buckingham for the cause. George Abbot had not been above playing a part in helping Buckingham to power in the first place, ignoring the warnings of the Queen that little good would come of such hypocrisy (**89**). Astute politician as he was, George Abbot made the mistake of offending the King over the notorious Essex marriage annulment* in 1613, which some say cost his brother Robert promotion to the see of Lincoln. A small flurry of appointments for Arminians was the obvious reward for the more obsequious behaviour of Neile and Andrewes at the hearings.

The rise of Buckingham brought a random factor into Church politics, before he sided clearly with Arminians much later in his career. But it was James's pursuit of a Spanish match for his son, coupled with the start of the Thirty Years War in 1618, which first unsettled the King's *via media**. Archbishop Abbot was strongly identified with the 'Protestant Cause' and those who called for James to do all in his power to aid his son-in-law, Frederick, the Elector Palatine. He called for strong measures against Catholics at home and abroad. Fearful that Abbot would encourage the clergy to preach a Protestant crusade, under the guise of collecting money for the Palatinate, James turned to Richard Neile and the compliant Arminians* to ensure restraint. Only when royal policy changed again in 1624 did they jump on the parliamentary bandwagon calling for war.

In the final analysis, however, the most significant changes in this period may not have stemmed from the shifting balance of fortunes of different factions within the Church, but from the new relationship which was slowly being forged between the clerical estate in general and the state. By allowing clergymen to return to holding high government office, James was setting the clock back to policies pursued before the Reformation. And it was not only in

England that bishops returned to the Privy Council. The change must have seemed even more dramatic in Scotland, where for a brief period before the Council was reconstituted in 1610, the entire Scottish bench of two archbishops and eleven bishops had a theoretical right to sit on the Council. This never happened in practice, but the very idea must have stuck in the gullets of Scottish Presbyterians* who had only comparatively recently had to swallow the re-imposition of bishops in Scotland. And it was not only bishops in central government who began to relish secular power. Around 1616 it became apparent that ordinary clergymen were being picked in greater numbers than ever before to sit on Commissions of the Peace*. Only ten clergymen below the rank of dean served as a Justice of the Peace in 1604, but the figure had shot to seventy-eight by 1622.

So we are left with mixed messages about the reign of James I. On the one hand, his policies seem wise and even-handed, his appointments equally so. Yet it is possible to argue that he bequeathed a legacy of problems to Charles I far worse than that which he inherited from Elizabeth. By encouraging and aiding the clergy, he fanned lay fears of their influence in government. By acknowledging divisions within the Church and playing factions off against one another, he aided and abetted the rise of the potentially dangerous Arminian* party. Even if he personally felt able to control their excesses, his failing health in the latter years of his reign, coupled with his need for their support over his foreign and domestic policy, undoubtedly left the Arminians in a strong position in 1625. If George Abbot had been an inspired choice as Archbishop of Canterbury in 1611, James did little to help him to survive as a dominant voice at the Court of Charles I. It is now a matter of historical debate as to how far James I, or George Abbot, may be held responsible for the ills of the Church which materialised later, but it is certain that they handed to Charles I a very confusing state of affairs.

Charles I

The reign of Charles I brought a different kind of royal involvement in the Church, but the topic is deeply controversial. Whilst James appears to have been a good Calvinist at heart, his son's religious stance is less clear (**42**). Some commentators emphasise his craving for outward 'order and decency' and match this to other features of Court life of the period; others point to the fact that he died a martyr to his concept of the Church of England. There is no denying that Charles was a deeply religious man. Nor is there any doubt that he felt strongly committed to the established Church of England. Problems arise when we attempt to assess the extent and nature of his personal control (**54, 128, 185**).

Where James tried to be even-handed in his Church appointments and fought to maintain a *via media**, Charles was much more partisan. Arminian* controversies had surfaced more openly in England by the time of his coronation, but it was William Laud who presided over that event, and by that date, the outspoken Arminian Richard Montagu had become a royal chaplain. Rapid promotions followed for prominent Arminians, and a flurry of appointments in 1628 led to rows in Parliament. A year earlier Bishops Neile and Laud had been appointed to the Privy Council. By 1633, although both had been branded as enemies of true religion in the parliamentary session of 1629, they were Archbishops of York and Canterbury respectively.

The effect of these partisan policies on ordinary people is debatable, but there is no denying that old-fashioned Puritans* must have felt under great pressure. The 'Proclamation for Peace and Quiet in the Church' issued in 1626 was ostensibly aimed at all sides, but was used in reality to quash Protestant complaints about the Arminians* [**doc. 11**]. Censorship laws were tightened. In the 1630s, writers like William Prynne, Henry Burton, John Bastwick, and Alexander Leighton were harshly dealt with for their criticism of the religious establishment. Sympathisers within that establishment, like Bishops Davenant, Morton and Hall, found their own freedom of action curtailed. The definition of a 'Puritan' had subtly changed [**docs 12** and **26**].

James I may have been happy to lay down general policy, but he did not relish the day-to-day detail of administration. Charles, on the other hand, seems to have gone about his duties extremely conscientiously, almost obsessively. This has posed difficulties for historians, for should we see his close interest in Church affairs as evidence that he was personally in charge, or should we merely assume that his counsellors gave him a lot of paperwork (**150**)? A proclamation of 1629 concerning the physical condition of parish churches led to a major church restoration campaign in some parts of the country; another order of 1629 required annual reports from bishops. Charles's marginal comments on these reports suggest that he took a keen interest in these affairs, but it is difficult to deduce whether he was really the originator of the policies in question, and how far his comments cloaked the actions of others with royal authority.

It may be difficult to pin down the King's private beliefs, but he left few in doubt about his concern for 'order and decency' in worship, and his faith in a certain group of theologians to carry out his policies, at least until 1640. Laud was the King's right-hand man, and practically all the appointments of the 1630s were of people known to contemporaries as 'Arminians'*, whatever the problems of definition which surround that term. Charles placed such a value on his Church that he eventually died for it, much as Lancelot Andrewes had predicted in a private conversation in 1623. It is ironic that the first King brought up in the Church of England should have died for it, but at least he accepted the ultimate consequences of being Supreme Governor of the Church.

It is often assumed that Charles brought about the downfall of his state for the sake of his views of the Church. More recently, however, it has been argued that the Church only fell because of its close identification with his particular state (**117**). James I had led the way in giving clergymen more secular power; they served as Justices of the Peace, took charge of government enquiries, and were even, in one case, appointed as a Lord Lieutenant with control over the local militia. Most important, they acted as key royal advisers in the Privy Council, and hence had an automatic right to sit as judges in the Court of Star Chamber. Under Charles I, Neile, Laud, and Juxon were influential councillors, and in 1634, John Spottiswood, Archbishop of St Andrews, was appointed Lord Chancellor in Scotland. When William Juxon, Bishop of London, was appointed Lord Treasurer in England in 1636, it appeared to many that the clerical estate had regained a prominence only enjoyed before under Cardinal Wolsey. Meanwhile, bishops in the provinces played a strong role in local government and were in a position, through their annual reports, to provide information of great use to the state. The clergy gave their own financial support to the Crown, but they also encouraged others to comply with the state, as in the celebrated cases of the Forced Loan of 1627 and subsequently Ship Money. It was later claimed in the Long Parliament that 'our bishops have so long played the Governors, as they have forgotten how to play the priests' (**30,** p. 431).

Charles I may have eventually met his downfall precisely because he possessed a much stronger Church than had existed in 1604 – stronger not in the sense that people felt more committed to the doctrine and organisation of the Church of England, but because the bishops and clergy held greater trappings of power than before and because they had more influence on government policies. Archbishops Neile and Laud were known by many as enemies of Parliament, and Laud had argued against calling one in 1628, claiming that 'the Church is too weak already. If it had more power, the King might have more obedience and service' (**28,** vi, p. 245). Recent interpretations of the events of this period have stressed the royal supremacy and taken what the various monarchs did and said at face value (**128**). This places too much faith in theory and ignores the nuances of what actually happened in practice. We should not under-estimate how far the clergy in general, and Arminians* in particular, had subtly altered the balance of power by 1640, something which was acknowledged by the wave of criticism which swept over all aspects of the Church in the early 1640s.

3 The Episcopate, 1570–1640

There were twenty-three English and four Welsh sees during this period, divided for the purposes of ecclesiastical administration into two provinces: Canterbury and York. The latter, comprising York, Durham, Chester, Carlisle, and Sodor & Man, covered extensive territory, but was clearly the junior partner of the two provinces. So, in theory, there should have been twenty-seven bishops (including the two archbishops) at any one time, all bar Sodor & Man entitled to sit in the House of Lords. The word 'theory' matters, for in practice, particularly during the reign of Elizabeth, sees were often left vacant, or in the case of Gloucester and Bristol between 1562 and 1589 held *in commendam**(that is, in association with another living). Vacancies were most common in the reign of Elizabeth, and only in 1627–28 did a number of sees stand vacant for more than one year under the Stuarts. This reflects the new respect with which bishops were treated by the Crown after 1603.

Individual dioceses varied enormously. Five were of relatively recent origin: Peterborough, Chester, Oxford, Bristol, and Gloucester. Cut out of some of the larger medieval dioceses, they had not been particularly well endowed (**157**). All of the 'new' foundations yielded incomes of less than £500 per annum, well below the best sees like Winchester, Canterbury, and Ely, which were worth more than £2,000 per annum. Bishops were still rich enough to be powerful, but the vast majority commanded incomes of less than £1,000 per annum. Whilst these are crude figures based on old valuations and take no account of fluctuations in land values and rents, all of the dioceses posed economic headaches for their respective bishops as inflation bedevilled the sixteenth century and thus set the tone for retrenchment later. Reputations varied, and some dioceses, like Lincoln, were in decline after years of medieval splendour; others, like Ely and Salisbury, were coveted retirement billets. Southern dioceses close to London could be a useful start to a career; Wales could mean oblivion (**65, 66**)!

The bishops who held these sees have also enjoyed mixed reputations. The Elizabethan episcopate* found themselves heaped with obloquy in the *Martin Marprelate* tracts of the 1580s; Caroline bishops suffered a similar fate from the pen of William Prynne. More recently, the Jacobean episcopate has been singled out for abuse, but all this is changing as propaganda and facts get slowly disentangled. Any criteria by which these bishops may be judged should acknowledge that they were faced with great difficulties, stubborn monarchs, and changing expectations. They were required to perform a wide spectrum of functions from spiritual leader to state civil servant, and it was always difficult to get the balance right (**148**).

Each bishop had his own episcopal style, and time and circumstances, such as the needs of a particular diocese, could affect the choice of priorities (**149**). Bishops might encounter very different expectations, say, in a diocese like Durham with a large number of Catholic recusants*, as opposed to one like Norwich where there were many Puritans*. All bishops would be expected to show pastoral concern for their flock, clerical and lay. This would imply regular preaching, the offering of Christian hospitality to local gentry and those in need, apt selection of lay officials, and moral leadership. Similar considerations would apply where diocesan clergy were concerned. Bishops would again be expected to lead by example, examine ordination candidates carefully, and provide patronage and support. While diocesan visitations* carried a large inspectorial function, they also afforded opportunities to get to know the clergy in the receptions which invariably followed. Diocesan synods* could serve a similar purpose (**58**).

Although many placed the pastoral role of the bishop high in their priorities, there is no doubt that the tasks faced by bishops grew increasingly complex over the period. It was one thing to be a good theologian, give excellent sermons, and write scholarly books – as so many bishops did. It was another to be able to cope with estate management in an economy going through difficult times. Diocesan surveys, productive leasing policies, property improvements – particularly with regard to diocesan residences and churches – all demanded shrewd business skills. Sound management of the full panoply of Church courts which operated in any diocese was no mean feat. Such vital, if mundane, administrative concerns could often clash with the more expected roles required of a theologian. Activities varied greatly according to the abilities of each individual bishop. It is tempting to judge any group of bishops by their literary output or charismatic preaching, but mundane administrative skills were also needed in the Church. There was always debate over what was expected of a model bishop [**docs 14** and **15**].

At a national level, bishops played a leading role in Convocation*, but the surviving records of that body reveal scant information about more than the basic Canons* (**26**). At the same time as Convocation was in session, all the bishops (except Sodor & Man), would be expected to take their place in the House of Lords. Research on this particular role of the episcopal bench suggests that such work was valued highly by most bishops. Michael Graves has shown that Elizabethan bishops were conscientious but, owing to vacancies, 'there was never a full complement of bishops when parliament met'. (**60**) The situation improved greatly under James I. In the parliaments held between 1604 and 1621, there were generally twenty bishops in attendance, allowing for six absentees, some of whom did not sit and sent proxies. Whereas you could generally expect three-quarters of the bishops to attend the House, you could rarely find half the lay peers. It would not, however, be true to say that bishops, as a rule, were popular in either house of Parliament. They were looked down on by many of the lay peers in the Lords, and viewed as an anachronism by many members of the Commons (**58, 196**).

The attendance of bishops at Court was not encouraged by Elizabeth, so it aroused comment when 'Court bishops' were identified soon after 1603. Bishops such as Andrewes, Bilson, and Neile became favourites of the new King, because they were excellent preachers, intellectuals, or simply good company. It has already been noted that James promoted several bishops to his Privy Council where Elizabeth had only ever allowed one – namely, Whitgift. But other bishops found their services required for the central ecclesiastical courts, special commissions, and aiding the King in his literary endeavours (**58**). Partly by virtue of proximity to the capital, the bishoprics of Winchester, Rochester, and London supplied several courtiers, but other bishops could be drawn into the net. The offices of Royal Almoner and Clerk of the Closet supplied residences and excuses for Court service for some; royal chaplains took their turns on duty. Yet the pull of the Court should not be exaggerated. It has been calculated that only eleven out of twenty-eight Jacobean bishops between 1610 and 1625 could be classified as 'Court bishops', and of those only four ever stayed with the Court for more than four months in a year (**58**).

Elizabethan bishops

According to Hugh Trevor-Roper, Elizabethan bishops were dull but dutiful (**190**). In fact, the first generation of bishops had grave doubts about their role, and these were still noticeable when Grindal was suspended in 1577. Men like Curteys of Chichester were in the forefront of promoting the very activities which the Queen had ordered to be suppressed; many in the ecclesiastical hierarchy had great sympathy with Grindal's stand over prophesy-ings*. These bishops saw themselves as 'first amongst equals' in the fight for continuing Protestant reformation. They faced abuse from all sides, but from what little we know, most have a reason-able record given the problems they faced.

A change in the episcopal bench became noticeable in the late 1570s and can probably be dated from the appointments of John Aylmer to London and John Whitgift to Worcester in 1577. These men took their status very seriously and were far more authori-tarian in their attitudes. They made greater demands on both laity and clergy for uniformity and discipline above all else: tender consciences would no longer be tolerated. When Grindal died in 1583, John Whitgift was a natural successor as Archbishop of Canterbury. A campaign for greater uniformity was undertaken, and some ministers left the Church at this juncture rather than subscribe to the Three Articles* [**doc. 7**]. The work of the Court of High Commission, once aimed chiefly at the discovery of recusants*, was now widened in scope to include dissident Puritans*. This prompted William Cecil, Lord Burghley, to liken its role to that of the 'Romish Inquisition' and later inspired the cartoons of Thomas Stirry [**doc. 28**].

Slowly but surely the character of the Elizabethan bench was changing. One bitter acknowledgement of this can be seen in the way in which bishops like Cooper of Winchester were denounced in the *Martin Marprelate* tracts of the 1580s. Power now lay with disciplinarians like Freke, Piers, and Aylmer, who were under instructions from their Queen to brook no nonsense. Younger theologians of similar temperament like Richard Bancroft, Samuel Harsnett, and Anthony Watson were on hand and eager to assume episcopal responsibilities. In the 1590s, the writings of Richard Hooker set the seal on this new confidence amongst the senior clergy. The day of the administrator was dawning and the stress on the preaching and pastoral functions of the episcopate*, although still dominant amongst the bench, was at last being questioned.

The Jacobean episcopate*

Thanks largely to a celebrated article by Hugh Trevor-Roper, the Jacobean episcopate has had a bad press. They have been characterised as 'worldly, courtly, talented place hunters who betrayed the principles of the English Church' (**190,** p. 571). Trevor-Roper highlighted the nature of episcopal appointments made between 1610 and 1628, claiming that James 'did not choose men for his jobs, but bestowed jobs on his men' (**190,** p. 573). To put it bluntly, 'the court of James I was a court of sponges' (**190,** p. 574). The appointments were largely unworthy, particularly so after the rise of Buckingham. Singled out for condemnation by Trevor-Roper was Archbishop George Abbot ('simply indifferent, negligent, secular') (**190,** p. 575), and John Williams, whose appointment as Lord Keeper in 1621 marked him out as a typical clerical careerist in Court clothes. The best Trevor-Roper would say of the Jacobean bishops was that they were patrons of learning, intelligent and witty company; he itemised Thornborough the mineralogist, Goodman the philosopher, and Donne the poet (despite the trifling fact that Donne never became a bishop!).

The debate sparked off by Trevor-Roper relates to that on the origins of the British Civil War. For Trevor-Roper, the Church was being assailed by Puritans* of the 'left', and of the 'right', and it eventually succumbed to both. First, the weakness of Abbot as archbishop created a backlash when Laud succeeded him in 1633. Laud's work, in turn, triggered a true Puritan backlash during the Interregnum. Under this analysis, Laud and Puritans were equally frustrated by Abbot's long tenure of office. Given that Laud, in his anxiety to carry out much-needed reforms, caused deep offence and thereby helped to provoke war, Abbot and his colleagues must bear some of the blame because they 'betrayed' the Church at an earlier stage.

Variations of this argument still exist today, and indeed one way of seeing different interpretations of this period is to study how the Archbishops of Canterbury have been viewed – namely, Grindal, Whitgift, Bancroft, Abbot, and Laud. This is an alternative to assessing events by reigning monarchs. If Grindal and Abbot are seen as heroic in their efforts to preside over a broad Church, then Whitgift, Bancroft, and Laud fall into place as the villains, who were dangerous, narrow-minded disciplinarians. If, on the other hand, these three are seen as sound, realistic churchmen who simply sought a modicum of religious unity and did their best to ensure the survival of the Church as an institution, then Grindal and Abbot fall into the guise of innocent, naïve, or negligent individuals. This exercise has the merit of forcing us to examine how we interpret, consciously or not, significant dates. While some historians highlight 1583, 1610, and 1633 as critical for the Church, others prefer to emphasise 1603 and 1625.

Needless to say, Trevor-Roper's extravagant claims did not go unchallenged (**164, 182**). There were many obvious flaws to his case. The Jacobean bishops cited were not really much different from their Elizabethan predecessors or Caroline successors; they were all well-educated, worthy citizens (**164**). Abbot played his part in strengthening the administration of the Church and protecting its courts from the attacks of common lawyers (**124**). His archiepiscopate is now viewed in a very favourable light by some historians (**148, 145, 161**). Trevor-Roper's selection of a 'Jacobean' period between 1610 and 1628 seems a trifle odd, particularly as Bancroft was also a Jacobean archbishop! The attack on the patronage system was central to his case, but was this really so atypical of early modern government? Few would now argue that Court favourites really exercised a strong, malign influence on Church affairs. Many of the 'Laudians' seen by Trevor-Roper as praiseworthy and earnest in the 1630s had been promoted in the 1620s partly through Buckingham, as indeed was Laud himself. Some of Buckingham's early forays into Church patronage may have been unworthy, such as his backing for Snowden and Bayly, but his later 'capture' by the Arminians* is completely overlooked by Trevor-Roper (**89**).

Recent research on the Jacobean episcopate* has shifted the terms of the debate to the problems discussed at the outset of this chapter (**58**). By what criteria should we judge these bishops? How were the roles they were expected to play changing? And whose perceptions have dominated the historiographical debate – those of later Anglicans or those of Puritans*? Kenneth Fincham has shown that the Jacobean bishops were far from negligent, and very few of them could be counted as courtiers (**58**). Non-residence of bishops has been exaggerated, and they seem, by and large, to have played a full part in the day-to-day administration of their dioceses. Even the small band of 'Court bishops' that has now been usefully identified spent most of their summers in their dioceses, usually on visitation*. Perhaps most important, Kenneth Fincham has found that the ideal of the preaching pastor, beloved of Thomas Fuller, remained a dominant one, even though a significant number of bishops now chose alternative models, urged on by the likes of John Cosin [**docs 14** and **15**].

What is most important about the reign of James I is that it bestowed greater status and prestige on the bishops than they had enjoyed under Elizabeth. They were now accepted and valued members of the Court and government. This could and did lead to problems of priorities, and it is probable that both Abbot and Williams strayed too far at times into the role of civil servant. Worldly bishops could be found, of course, like the obsequious Thomas Bilson and the more notorious Lewis Bayly, known in Wales as 'the Bishop of Banghoore', despite the fact that he was the author of the best-selling *Practice of Piety* (**58**, p. 32). Yet the overwhelming number of bishops seem to have been worthy spiritual leaders and capable administrators. If things were starting to go wrong, it was not due to inappropriate selection procedures and ill-qualified bishops, but to the emergence of the Arminian* party, which even by 1625 held important dioceses like Durham (**118**).

The Caroline episcopate*

The dust may be settling on long-running arguments about the Jacobean episcopate, but controversy now envelops the reputation of their Caroline successors. The problems relate chiefly to the question of Arminianism*, which is discussed elsewhere (pp. 33–46). Suffice it to say here that much hinges on the best way of characterising the religious policies pursued by the Caroline bishops, the manner in which those policies were implemented, and the matter of who was really in charge – Archbishop Laud or Charles I.

There is no denying that the selection of bishops took on a more partisan hue after the accession of Charles I. Apart from one or two exceptions to the rule, such as Barnabas Potter's appointment to Carlisle in 1629, the bulk of episcopal appointments between 1625 and 1640 were from the group known to contemporaries as Arminians*. Some of these were doubly controversial appointments, for Richard Montagu, who gained Chichester in 1628 and was later elevated to Norwich, and Roger Manwaring, who gained St David's in 1635, had both been complained of in Parliament. Nevertheless, it is necessary to be cautious before assuming that the episcopal bench of the 1630s was necessarily more united than any of its predecessors, whether by common theological interests or abilities. Good Calvinists from an earlier era, like Thomas Morton, Joseph Hall, and John Davenant, retained their sees. Laud's arch-rival John Williams may have been stripped of his Lord Keepership, but he remained a thorn in Laud's side as Bishop of Lincoln, until the unusual step was taken of suspending him in 1637. He bounced back to gain York in 1641, helped by his status as a prominent victim of the Laudian ascendancy.

William Laud became Bishop of London in 1628, and many historians refer to bishops appointed after that date and before 1640 as 'Laudian'. This term needs to be treated with great caution, for it implies much greater unity than was probably the case. Just as it is wise to remember that there were different types of Calvinists, so too, not all 'Laudians' or 'Arminians*' were necessarily the same. John Howson and Samuel Harsnett were Arminians who held important sees after 1628, but they were never part of the Durham House group* led by Neile and Laud. Equally, it is possible that several of the appointments made in the 1630s may properly be described as 'Laudian', only in the sense that careerists adapted to the way the wind was blowing, even if they did not necessarily share Laud's theological outlook. This would apply to bishops like Robert Wright and John Towers (**118, 150**).

There is one way in which the Caroline episcopate* may have been more united than its predecessors. If our new dominant image of a Jacobean bishop is of a preaching pastor, that of his Caroline equivalent is of a busy administrator, responding frantically to a constant flow of orders from Lambeth and Whitehall. Royal orders in 1629 and 1633 placed heavy duties on the bishops: they were required to observe better residence in their dioceses, regulate the work of lecturers*, carry out more efficient leasing policies, and to provide annual reports for the archbishop and the King [**doc. 13**]. Campaigns were organised for the restoration and 'beautification' of parish churches (**148, 150**). Bishops found themselves appointed to commissions dealing with local poor relief, much to the chagrin of some of the local gentry who saw the matter as their preserve. Meanwhile, the trend to employ bishops in high state office was maintained with the appointment of Juxon as Lord Treasurer in 1636. It is a wonder that the bishops ever found time to preach under this regime!

No matter what label is used for these bishops, there is no doubt that the policies pursued caused irreparable harm to the Church and helped to bring about the British Civil War. Patrick Collinson has gone so far as to describe Laud as 'the greatest calamity ever visited upon the Church of England' (**47**, p. 90). In the Long Parliament after 1640, bishops were charged with encouraging their ministers 'to despise the temporal Magistracy, the nobles, and gentry of the land, to abuse the subjects and live contentiously with their neighbours'. They were accused of labouring to 'overthrow and diminish the power of Parliament' [**doc. 27**], yet clergymen generally were also taunted for studying 'the statutes more than the Ten Commandments' (**2**, p. 10). Although little different from many of their Elizabethan and Jacobean predecessors, bishops associated with Laud were scorned and derided for their low social origins. This did not matter when bishops could still be ranked amongst the godly, but it recalled memories of Cardinal Wolsey, the son of a butcher, when they were accused of betraying the Church in the 1630s. Feelings ran so high in the Long Parliament that bishops were soon expelled from the Lords, and episcopacy* itself was abolished in 1646.

The charges carried so much force because of the way in which people had seen the bishops and clergy in general behave in the 1630s. The dissolution of Parliament in 1629 may not have signalled an 'eleven years' tyranny' as the Whigs once had us believe, but that concept still conveys useful images about the episcopal style of Laud and some of his colleagues. Neile and Laud pursued their policies with great vigour and carried out wide-ranging metropolitical visitations* of their respective provinces between 1632 and 1635 [**docs 22** and **23**]. Laud extended his, controversially, to cover the universities of Oxford and Cambridge (**43, 186**). With great bureaucratic zeal, they sought to ensure that ministers and laity were obeying all rules of the Church. Potentially subversive lectureships* were suppressed, lay impropriators* urged to return property to the Church, and a select band of Feoffees for Impropriations* was disbanded. Even the rights of foreign congregations worshipping in this country were strictly curtailed, to ensure that English people could not resort to alternative Protestant services. This policy has been well characterised as showing an obsessive concern with 'uniformity', where all that had been sought before had been 'unity'.

Voluminous annual reports, letters, and larger volumes of visitation* material tempt one to think that bishops like Richard Neile, Matthew Wren, and William Piers were more efficient than many of their predecessors. If this was really the case, their success owed much to the way in which they mobilised the support of a number of civil lawyers*. Sir Nathaniel Brent, Sir John Lambe, and William

Easdall were critical figures in carrying out reforms in the 1630s. This fact was not lost on William Prynne, who complained bitterly that on moving to a new diocese, a bishop would take with him 'seven other spirits, as bad, or more wicked themselves (to wit, Archdeacons, Chancellors, registrars, Apparitors, Household Chaplains, Secretaries and private informers) who reside either near or with them in their diocese' (**33,** p. 9). Prynne's concern was amply justified if one thinks of the entourage which surrounded Neile at Durham House* in the 1620s (**118, 148**).

If bishops were hardly popular figures at the start of this period, they had become the objects of virulent criticism by 1640. This owes much to the fact that the complex system of Court patronage, which had worked reasonably well under Elizabeth and James, broke down in the 1620s. The 'system' was disturbed not so much by Court favourites as by the appearance of a significant Church faction – namely, the Arminians*. Their progress had initially been impeded by the King's careful policy of balancing Calvinist and Arminian appointments, but when foreign affairs altered for the worst, their unstinting support for the Crown gave them the edge. After 1625, the policy of episcopal appointments was far more partisan, with one or two exceptions which serve merely to prove the rule. This faction was led by Bishops Neile and Laud, and was bound together by a mutual interest in Arminian theology.

4   Theological Disputes and Factional Politics

The Church of England may have been established by the Acts of Uniformity and Supremacy of 1559, and the Canons* of 1562/63, but it was a very curious Church in contemporary eyes, occupying an uncertain and ill-defined position. In its allegiance to the scriptures, creeds, and works of the early Christian Church it still claimed to be part of a broad and pure Catholic tradition. Notions of purgatory and transubstantiation had been condemned, but ceremonies such as the use of the cross in baptism, as well as the wearing of vestments* had been preserved. The seven orders of the Catholic ministry may have been cut to three – deacon, priest, and bishop – but that was still too many for some. Church courts remained and still administered canon law, while at the grass-roots, parishes were preferred to the 'new-fangled device' of Calvin's Presbyterian* system.

The authority of the Pope had been denied and the royal supremacy asserted in its stead. The number of sacraments had been reduced from seven to two, namely baptism and holy communion, though some Protestants still hankered after penance. The calendar of the Holy Year had been drastically reduced, along with all references to the Virgin Mary and the saints. In the churches themselves, furnishings had been cut to a minimum and the altar had become a movable communion table which often stood in the middle of the church. Church music was less elaborate than before the Reformation and the emphasis of the service was most definitely upon the minister and his sermon rather than on the priest as magician. The supremacy of the Bible was asserted over all other authorities like the Pope, Church Councils, and the commentaries of the early Christian Fathers*. Yet a Prayer Book had been retained – with many 'imperfections' as far as Puritans* were concerned – and the Canons* of the Church laid down in 1562/63 were likewise often ambiguous. Canon ten, for example, rejected free will, but Canon seventeen was vague about what was involved in predestination* and election*, issues which were to be controversial throughout this period (**126**).

Relations with foreign Protestant churches, both at home and abroad, offer one measure of the curious status of the Church of England; they were generally uneasy on both sides. Foreign theologians could not resist giving advice to old friends from the days of the Marian exile, and certainly many English Protestants still hoped for reform along Calvinist lines. There were disputes about technicalities such as the validity of ordination and holy orders: were ministers who had been ordained abroad qualified to serve in the English Church, where claims were made about apostolic succession? Many foreign Protestants, like Calvin's successor, Theodore Beza, criticised England's retention of bishops. Calvinism was the dominant brand of theology in the English Church at this stage, but there was obviously still quite a gulf when it came to organisation and discipline. Many of the early English Puritans* took comfort from their contacts abroad, but these became frowned upon by the authorities in the 1580s. The foreign theologians who now felt encouraged to come to England were people like Adrian Saravia, Peter Baro, and Anthony Corro, who were far from being hard-line Calvinists. Indeed, they led the questioning of key tenets of Calvinism, particularly those to do with the doctrine of grace (**82, 84, 85, 117, 118**).

Questions raised in the 1590s

It would be wrong to suggest that the 'Calvinist consensus' which was finally about to break in the 1590s was anything stronger than a 'common and ameliorating bond' uniting conformists and moderate Puritans*, or that it extended much beyond an educated elite (**192,** p. 121). Nor did the existence of this bond preclude fierce disputes between churchmen over theological matters as well as more practical issues of Church government (**136**). Until the 1590s, many of the debates could be characterised as being held between 'credal' and 'experimental' predestinarians*, to borrow terms employed by R. T. Kendall and Peter Lake (**82, 166**). 'Experimental' predestinarians 'wanted to place their view of predestination, election* and assurance at the centre of their practical divinity', while 'credal' Calvinists were more moderate souls who 'had no impulse to take the doctrine into the popular pulpit or to derive a view of the Christian community from it' (**166,** pp. 39–40). Here lies one way of distinguishing between moderate and extreme Calvinists. Nicholas Tyacke stresses the role of Arminians*, who appeared in the 1590s, precisely because they were 'anti-Calvinists', who broke through the shared belief system of the times (**118**).

The questioning of the Church, which at the start of the period was largely the prerogative of Puritans* and Presbyterians*, was gathering momentum in other quarters. John Whitgift, aided now by Sir Christopher Hatton at Court, was happy to gain allies in the fight to discredit Puritans by associating them with the more extreme Presbyterians. According to Peter Lake, 'the clerical ideologues of this faction inserted the *jure divino* defence of episcopacy* into the centre of the propaganda effort' (**85,** p. 210). Richard Bancroft typifies the two-pronged nature of the attack with his sermon delivered in 1589 in defence of the despised office of bishop, and his later, trenchant *Dangerous Positions and Proceedings* published against Presbyterians in 1593. But there were many issues on which anti-Calvinists now chose to speak out against their increasingly discredited opponents. Samuel Harsnett had preached boldly against the harsh doctrine of predestination* in 1584. That issue surfaced again in Cambridge disputes in 1595. Theologians like Lancelot Andrewes and John Overall began to quote freely from the writings of the early Christian Fathers*. Disputes erupted over the sanctity of Sundays. It was claimed that Puritans misused the practice of exorcism in order to whip up religious fervour. In 1598, John Howson dared to cast doubts on the much-vaunted efficacy of preaching (**83, 84, 101, 118**).

Easily the dominant thinker behind these debates was Richard Hooker. The first parts of his magisterial *Laws of Ecclesiastical Polity* appeared in 1593. Published eventually in eight books, the first four came out in 1593, book five in 1597, books six and eight posthumously in 1648 and 1651. Book seven first appeared in Bishop Gauden's edition of Hooker's *Works* in 1662. Hooker's stress on reason and the concept of *adiaphora*, or 'things indifferent', provided the spur for re-interpretation of the nature of the Church of England along lines scarcely envisaged in 1559. It was Hooker who not only defended the ramshackle mixture noted above, but actually made it seem like a divinely ordained compromise. With this spirit abroad there is little wonder that some of the theologians of the day began to appear quite strident in their defence of say, episcopacy* or ceremonies (**84**).

Controversy over the doctrine of grace

The issue which eventually galvanised most theologians into angry reaction was the complicated doctrine of grace, involving difficult topics like election*, predestination* and the problem of Calvinist assurance*. The thorny questions of whether Christ died for all men, and whether the elect were certain, or 'assured' in their faith, or liable to fall from grace, dominated Cambridge debates in the 1590s. When William Barrett, a follower of Peter Baro, Lady Margaret Professor of Divinity, preached a sermon for his Bachelor of Divinity degree in the summer of 1595, he denied the certainty of assurance. There was uproar at this 'Popery' and Barrett was forced to recant. It was this affair which prompted Whitgift to issue the nine Lambeth Articles* in November of that year. Some argue he did this in an effort to heal the breach; others feel it was a move to flush out innovators, for Whitgift was at heart a sound Calvinist. It was Queen Elizabeth who stepped in to call a halt to the controversy by demanding that the articles be withdrawn [**doc. 16**] (**83, 101, 118, 194**).

The damage, however, had been done and the Lambeth Articles* stand as a watershed in the history of the English Church. They express ideas which were possibly once held by the majority of English Protestants, but which were never ratified as principles of the English Church, despite various attempts to do so in the seventeenth century. The fracas drew Peter Baro into the open in defence of Barrett, but led directly to his retirement. Victory, however, did not go to the rigid Calvinists at Cambridge, for although the orthodox Thomas Playfere replaced Baro as Lady Margaret Professor of Divinity, the controversial figure of John Overall succeeded William Whitaker, the Puritan* Master of St John's, as Regius Professor of Divinity. Moreover, Richard Clayton, another member of Baro's circle, had already succeeded Whitaker at St John's in a hotly disputed mastership election. According to Peter Lake it was 'in 1595/6 [that] the foundations of high Elizabethan protestantism started to crumble' (**83**, p. 239).

John Overall went on to become the champion of the anti-Calvinist cause in Cambridge. He was elected Master of St Catharine's College in 1598 and sparked off great controversy in the next few years with his views on assurance* and perseverance*. The Commencement degree ceremonies of 1600 were the occasion of some of the bitterest rows, when Overall clashed with other examiners over doctoral candidates and their theses. A foreigner visiting Cambridge at the time noted how the Moderator (Playfere) made a 'violent attack upon his colleague' (Overall) at the ceremonies. Apparently, Playfere 'belittled his theory concerning the Patriarchs, he undermined his arguments, and then he pressed home his own point with so much animus that the other man went quite red with mortification' (**19,** p. 99). No wonder this degree ceremony stands out in the history of Cambridge (**101**).

The Hampton Court Conference* and the Canons* of 1604

In 1603 Jacobus Arminius was appointed Professor of Theology at Leyden University, but the views which came to be associated with his name had already been hotly disputed in Cambridge and were about to move into a wider public arena (**160, 171**). Once seen as rather a waste of time, the Hampton Court Conference is now regarded in a more constructive light (**118, 135, 139, 144**). English Arminians*, as we now call them, were present at the conference amongst the select band of invited deans, for they were not yet bishops. They must have been well pleased when Puritan* demands for the publication of the Lambeth Articles* were rejected at the conference. And they were soon to discover, in Bancroft, an archbishop who was more sympathetic to their cause than the recently deceased Whitgift. Bancroft had once expressed the opinion that 'I live in obedience therefore I am of the elect hopefully' – which was a much more sceptical position than the orthodox line: 'I am elect therefore if I sin I shall not be damned' (**197,** p. 79). He went on to steer 141 new Canons through the Convocation of 1604 and to launch a campaign for clerical conformity on his appointment as Archbishop of Canterbury in the autumn. It is significant that the Church, under its royal governor, was now headed by the man who had led the successful fight against Presbyterianism* in the 1590s [**doc. 7**].

In the words of Nicholas Tyacke, 'at Hampton Court anti-Calvinism received, for the first time, an airing at national level' and 'even more important, the Hampton Court Conference* was the last time when the predestinarian* controversy was handled, by English religious leaders, in an atmosphere largely free from continental influences' (**118,** p. 9). But Arminianism* was still a side issue at this conference and nothing was settled. Nor did the 141 Canons* of 1604 contain startling innovations. The nature of the royal supremacy was further spelled out, as were the conditions necessary for Church services. The lawful use of the cross in baptism was explained, but this was the only Canon to mention the debates at Hampton Court. Other complaints were not forgotten, however, for a large number of Canons dealt with the ordination and function of ministers and also with the operation of the Church courts. These Canons expanded on the Thirty-nine Articles of 1562/63. With their stress on Church furniture and the nature of divine service – Canon eighteen, for instance, called for all to be done decently with reverence and order – they have been heralded by some as the key to William Laud's policies in the 1630s [**doc. 20**]. Apparently, a separate order was drawn up which laid down instructions that lower clergy were not to handle deep, controversial matters of theology like predestination* in their sermons, thus prefiguring royal orders to that effect in 1622 and 1626.

Bancroft's subscription campaign* seems to have been quite effective in ridding the Church of remaining Puritan* dissidents, helped as he was by the personal intervention of James I, who put pressure on local bishops while out hunting in East Anglia (**180**). Extremists were to be shunned, but the fact that many returned to the fold is a tribute to the success of the King's policy of a *via media** and also a comment on how many bishops still gave tacit support to Puritans. Bancroft turned his attention to what some have called a major 'reconstruction' of the Church, which was really founded upon settled government and the continuation of much of the work started by Whitgift (**122**). The interests of the Church were defended stoutly against lay encroachments whether in the matter of Church property or rights in courts. And of course, in James I the bishops found an ally in their cause.

Theological faction fighting

It was George Abbot who injected new life into the theological disputes of the day. On his promotion to be Archbishop of Canterbury in 1611, he set about attacking some of the Arminian* theologians, particularly the rising generation at Oxford like William Laud, but not excluding older scholars like Howson either. Abbot was aided in this campaign by continental developments. Arminius had not made himself popular in the Netherlands and his cause had become entangled in politics. On his death in 1609, Conrad Vorstius was nominated to succeed to his chair at Leyden. Vorstius was an established scholar of the Remonstrant party, as the Arminians became known later in the Netherlands. Sadly for his reputation and promotion chances, Vorstius was also tainted with the opinions of Socinius, an Italian theologian who had questioned the divinity of Christ and hence the Holy Trinity, from whence we derive the name Socinian (**187**).

James I was drawn into the election* disputes surrounding Vorstius, and thanks largely to Abbot, Morton and Winwood – at that time ambassador in the Netherlands – formed a poor opinion of Arminian* views as potentially subversive. With James keen to project his image abroad as a wise Christian monarch, the last thing he needed was to be associated with the views of extremists. The King declared himself against Vorstius, and the whole affair served as a prelude to his later involvement in the Synod of Dort*. At home, Abbot and his brother Robert made life uncomfortable for their Arminian enemies. Laud's election to the Presidency of St John's College, Oxford, in 1611 was hotly contested, and in 1615 both Howson and Laud were called before the King to answer for inflammatory sermons. The situation was so uncertain that Laud apparently despaired of his career (**21, 43, 116**).

Political factors were now playing a strong part in the fortunes of those who espoused anti-Calvinist ideas. They had prospered under Bancroft because he needed clergymen who were prepared to be strong administrators and who shared his ideals about the nature of worship expounded in the 1604 Canons*. Lancelot Andrewes and John Overall provided the intellectual meat for this cause, writing influential liturgical tomes, while also working on the new translation of the Bible. Richard Neile emerged as the 'political' leader of the party, drawing heavily on his own position as one of the King's favourites. It was Neile who had helped ensure Laud's election at St John's and who also gained him a royal chaplaincy in that same year. Neile played a vital part in Laud's early career and maintained the latter's spirits when the future looked bleak (**21, 148**).

English Arminians* were fortunate that what they had to offer chimed in not only with Bancroft's interests, but also with those of the King. James desired a decent and orderly Church. Arminian theologians offered him a new sense of ritual and worship with their stress on fine Church music, appealing liturgy*, and ornate Church furnishings. Soon after his appointment as Dean of Gloucester in 1616, Laud pitched the Church into new controversy over the nature and position of the communion table. Laud ordered the altar, as he referred to it, to be placed at the east end of the Cathedral; his bishop, Miles Smith, was horrified. This concern for the altar adds a sacramental dimension to English Arminianism which was absent in the Netherlands. It shows how ideas from the 1590s fused with various practical ceremonial initiatives to create a distinctive English tradition within the shell of the Church of England.

But new political factors abroad soon affected the fortunes of the English Arminians*. The advent of the Thirty Years War in 1618 drove the King away from Calvinist counsellors who advocated English intervention. James chose Calvinist representatives to attend the Synod of Dort*, but at home he gave bishoprics to Andrewes, Overall, and, later, Harsnett. Richard Neile had already gained the key post of Bishop of Durham in 1617. These men offered unstinting support to the King as he faced great pressure to go to war and they ensured that sermons about the Palatinate did not become inflammatory.

One by-product of this period was a much more sympathetic approach to the Roman Catholic Church. Arminians* saw great value in the work of the early Christian Fathers* and in the ceremonial and liturgy of the Catholic Church. Increasingly, perhaps aided by the appearance on the English scene of converts like Antonio de Dominis, Archbishop of Spalato, they saw their own work in the context of a broader Catholic tradition. John Cosin produced *Hours of Prayer* for Court ladies because he feared they were being lured into Catholicism by its rich liturgical tradition. Richard Neile always employed his most intellectual chaplains in the task of persuading leading Catholic gentry of the error of their ways. Here we have a different approach to the task of evangelising: while hard-line Protestants affirmed that the Pope was Antichrist and the Roman Catholic Church fundamentally flawed, their Arminian opponents pointed to the many similarities between the two Christian churches, while acknowledging that union was out of the question. It is a moot point as to which strategy was the more successful, but it is certain that the attitude of the Arminians tainted them with grave suspicion, especially when they too lost people as converts, as in the famous cases of William Alabaster and Benjamin Carrier, both royal chaplains who 'defected' to Rome. It is significant that the collapse of the broad Calvinist consensus in the 1590s not only completed the identification of Presbyterianism* as a dangerous and subversive 'popular' novelty, but it also saw the start of splits within Protestant ranks about the dangers and evil of Rome.

Religion in Parliament

Religious issues were always on any Parliamentary agenda, but usually in the form of concern over the enforcement of recusancy* laws or reform of abuses within the Church of England, such as pluralism*, non-residence, and the Church courts (**104**). When matters of theology were raised, most members recognised the rights of Convocation*, thus when Richard Montagu's book *A New Gagg for an Old Goose* was discussed in 1624, the issue was referred to Archbishop Abbot. Petitions concerning Harsnett's ceremonial changes at Norwich were debated, but not related at the time to the Arminian*, proto-Catholic writings of Montagu (**183**).

The Commons felt less embarrassed in 1625, for in their opinion Montagu had flouted royal orders by publishing a second book, entitled *Appello Caesarem*. They did not yet know that Richard Neile and his chaplains, John Cosin and Francis White, had been closely involved in the production of that book; nor were they prepared for the fact that Charles I was so willing to be partisan in the affair and to place Richard Montagu under his protection by making him a royal chaplain. This may have marked the point when the balance between Calvinists and Arminians* within the Church of England finally shifted in favour of the latter.

In an effort to separate the Duke of Buckingham from the Arminians* and perhaps to demonstrate doctrinal failings to the King, the Calvinist nobility urged a conference between leading theologians which took place at Buckingham's London home, York House*, in February 1626 (**142**, **194**). The Arminians John Buckeridge, Francis White and John Cosin took on John Preston and Thomas Morton, two impeccable Calvinists, in what turned out to be a fairly sterile debate. The Earl of Pembroke remarked that 'none returned Arminians thence, save such who repaired thither with the same opinions'; Thomas Fuller later noted drily that 'these Conferences betwixt divines rather increase the differences than abate them' [**doc. 30**]. If the Hampton Court Conference* was a round-table debate, the York House Conference* marked the end of that free discourse. The conference settled nothing, theologically speaking, but the compact between Buckingham and the Arminians was sealed in the summer when they helped him become Chancellor of Cambridge University despite his great unpopularity in the recent Parliament.

A further mark of the significance of 1626 lies in the 'Proclamation for Peace and Quiet in the Church'* issued in June [**doc. 11**]. Ostensibly it called for moderation on all sides and should be seen in context with the earlier orders of 1622 [**doc. 10**]. A foreign ambassador took the proclamation at face value, and thought it 'meant to extinguish Arminianism* which has lately been spreading in this country' (**22**, p. 76). The more suspicious Bishop Davenant worried 'how far those of Durham House* will stretch the meaning thereof', and his fears were more apt. He had in mind Neile's London residence which had become a gathering place for so many Arminian hopefuls that it went by the name of 'Durham College' (**21**). The doyen of the Arminian party, Lancelot Andrewes, died in 1626, but William Laud took his place as Dean of the Chapel Royal. The year ended on a high note for Arminians when Neile consecrated* Francis White as Bishop of Carlisle at Durham House in December. The point was not lost on one contemporary, who pinned a note to the door, asking: 'Is an Arminian now made a bishop, and is a consecration translated from Lambeth to Durham House?' (**4**, vol I, pp. 179–80). John Cosin preached a significant sermon on the role of bishops on that occasion [**doc. 14**].

By 1628 Parliament was beginning to piece together more of the picture. Neile and Laud had been made Privy Councillors in 1627; when Abbot was sequestered* from office later that year, for refusing to support the Crown's right to collect a forced loan, they were effectively put in charge of the Church. In 1628 Neile was translated to Winchester. John Pym orchestrated trouble in the House of Commons, and after the King had accepted the Petition of Right he was presented with a remonstrance which named Neile and Laud as leaders of the Arminian* faction 'justly suspected to be unsound in their opinions that way' (**104**, pp. 384 and 396). This did not deter Charles from promoting Buckeridge to Ely, Laud to London, and Mountain to York in the summer. Most controversial, Richard Montagu, condemned in recent parliamentary sessions, was consecrated* Bishop of Chichester. Sees for Leonard Mawe and Walter Curle only enhanced the image of an Arminian take-over of the episcopal bench in 1628.

The assassination of the unpopular Buckingham in August 1628 enabled members of Parliament to concentrate on religious grievances. The King attempted to buy support by rescinding his sequestration* of Abbot and nominating the Calvinist Barnabas Potter to be Bishop of Carlisle. Yet the new parliamentary session of 1629 still turned into a stormy affair for the Arminians*. Pym and the sub-committee for religion had called for evidence from

41

around the country and had asked scholars like William Prynne to search university archives for evidence against Arminianism. An isolated Calvinist prebendary of Durham, Peter Smart, complained of ceremonial changes wrought at Durham. Others chimed in with stories of changes elsewhere. Neile was singled out, for 'though he hath leaped through many bishoprics, yet he hath left popery behind him' (**31,** p. 59). On 25 February, amidst wild scenes as the Speaker was held in his chair, three resolutions were read to the Commons, the first of which declared:

> Whosoever shall bring in innovation in Religion, or by favour or countenance, seek to extend or introduce Popery or Arminianism or other opinions disagreeing from the true and orthodox Church, shall be reputed a capital enemy to this Kingdom and Commonwealth. (**183,** p. 41)

It was all to no avail. The Arminians* had long since captured Cambridge and also the heart of the King. His appointments in 1629 reverted to their former partisan pattern, with Harsnett moving to York and White to Norwich. A proclamation calling for better maintenance of churches was issued in October and presaged one of the most outstanding campaigns of the 1630s. Likewise, royal orders of December 1629 heavily circumscribed the activities of lecturers* [**doc. 13**].

By the time Parliament came to these issues again in the 1640s, it was to attack boldly on the charge of Popery and not waste time with the niceties of theological dispute in which they had become ensnared in the 1620s. All too often, when faced with hostile questions in Parliament or at Court, people regarded as Arminians* – clearly noted as those of 'Durham House'* – escaped by claiming that they were unfamiliar with the works of the Dutch theologian: both Montagu and Neile did this. But the implementation of Arminian policies in the 1630s crystallised matters in the minds of many. Ceremony, liturgical* innovations, total identification of the clergy with the interests of the Crown: these were the issues at stake in the Long Parliament. There is a separate chapter on the 1630s, but this discussion of theology and worship remains to be completed by reference to the complex historiographical debate which centres on problems of nomenclature.

The problem of definition

The problem of definition has haunted historians because it was obviously a difficult matter for contemporaries. Parliament took a long time to identify what was going wrong with the Church from its point of view (**104, 118, 183**). Arminians*, likewise, took time to gain power in the Church, and emphases therefore changed only gradually. Because so much of their work came to fruition in the 1630s, they have often been called 'Laudians', a term discussed later. Suffice it to say here, this label scarcely seems to do the movement justice. It divorces events in the 1630s from any kind of theological rationale, concentrates on effects without also considering causes, and identifies these changes too closely with one man.

The term 'Anglican' has sometimes been used because it conveys a broad theological image and captures something of the solidification of the Elizabethan Settlement after Hooker (**98**). Yet this was not a term used widely by contemporaries. Historians who use it today apply it either to moderates like Thomas Fuller and Joseph Hall, who tried in vain to mediate between Arminians* and Calvinists, or to what they call 'parish Anglicans'. The latter group has been identified both by scholars studying the Interregnum, who note loyal adherence to the use of the Prayer Book long after it was technically forbidden, and also by historians who feel that the ceremonial changes of the 1630s may have appealed to groups still scarcely weaned from Catholicism (**97**).

'High Churchmen' is another historian's concept that seems to suit those who emphasised the sacerdotal* role of the priesthood. But it is vague, all-embracing, and yet also narrowly liturgical*. It conjures up some equally vague notion of 'Low Church'. These terms would not have made much sense to contemporaries, even though they are common parlance in the twentieth century. The word 'conservative' has been used by some historians, like Ronald Marchant, but once again there is the problem of opposites (**172**). The word is used in connection with Arminians* in much the sense that Peter Heylyn liked – namely, to conjure up a return to broad traditions lost at the Reformation. It is no accident that Heylyn wrote a history of the Reformation which established just such an innocuous view of events. But what about the legitimate position of moderate Calvinists who had ruled the roost for most of Elizabeth's reign? In the 1590s it was they who were the conservatives and the Arminians who were the innovators.

So much depends on one's perspective. Historians today are fighting many of the battles of the propagandists of the seventeenth century. Nicholas Tyacke stands accused of seeing things too much from the perspective of William Prynne and the injured Puritans* (**169**, **193**, **194**). Peter White has adopted much of Peter Heylyn's stance and sees the Puritans inventing an alibi for their own subversive activities (**194**). He disputes the notion that there was any doctrinal revolution, views Montagu as a much-maligned moderate, and feels that the 'Proclamation for Peace and Quiet' of 1626 was a sincere attempt to quell debate on all sides. According to White, the York House Conference* was simply another 'Puritan* attempt to push the formularies of the Church of England in a Protestant direction, and like previous attempts it failed' (**194**, p. 50). So we have versions of history which stress conflict and versions which stress consensus. While the dispute rages, it is no coincidence that several historians are turning their attention to the middle ground where Thomas Fuller and Joseph Hall once stood [**docs 19** and **30**]!

For the moment, use of the term 'Arminian'* seems sensible for a variety of reasons. Many problems over its use stem from confusion between the English and the Dutch variety; the former contained sacerdotal* and episcopalian* elements suited to English conditions; the latter laid claims to toleration. In England the Arminians gained power through alliance with the Crown; in the Netherlands Arminians lost because they had no such alliance with the Orange party. Unlike many of the other terms considered above, there is clear evidence that contemporaries used the word 'Arminianism'. Books were written with that title; leaders of the so-called Arminian faction were cited in Parliament; and there was even a good joke cracked by Bishop Morley which made sense to the populace. When asked what the Arminians held (meaning their theology), his witty reply was 'the best livings in England'.

English Arminians* may have started out with strong interests in theological controversies and a view of the nature of the Church which derived from their readings in the Church Fathers* as well as their interest in liturgy*. Any definition of them, however, needs to take into account the way in which they gained power. They skilfully took advantage of the factional politics of the Courts of James and Charles, and had successfully hijacked the Church and universities by the late 1620s. It is a comment on this evolving definition that a chapter which started with discussion of apparently minor points about the theology of grace should have moved to consider Court faction fighting, religion in Parliament, and the nature of the Church of England.

5   A Clerical Profession?

Rectors*, vicars*, curates*, chaplains, and lecturers* formed the backbone of the clerical profession – along with a small number of favoured deans, archdeacons, prebendaries, and others of the cosseted cathedral clergy, who probably cherished episcopal ambitions (**138**). The majority of the clergymen of this period served their allotted timespan in one or more of the 9–10,000 parishes of England and Wales. They were expected to perform an increasing variety of functions – to satisfy changing lay expectations, uphold the social order, encourage obedience and loyalty to the Crown, and, of course, to provide and conduct Church services. Just as the notion of a 'model' bishop was much debated during this period, so too was that of the ideal clergyman. It was said of Henry Hammond that:

> In the discharge of his ministerial function, he satisfied not himself in diligent and constant preaching only; (a performance wherein some of late have fancied all religion to consist;) but much more conceived himself obliged to the offering up the solemn daily sacrifice of Prayer for his people, administering the Sacraments, relieving the poor, keeping hospitality, reconciling of differences amongst neighbours, visiting the sick, catechising the youth. (**13**, p. 162)

Given such a list, it is not surprising that historians have found much to discuss about the work of the parish clergy. The debates have touched upon clerical/lay relations, anti-clericalism, education and a sense of vocation, status, living standards, political associations, not to mention the part played by the clergy in the continuing Protestant reformation (**100, 133, 147, 153, 154, 155, 158**)!

Many questions about the changing role of the clergy in society have become inextricably linked in recent historical writing with the claim that the early modern period saw the emergence of several 'professions' (**100**). Lawyers spring most readily to mind, but by the mid-seventeenth century most clerics were university graduates, many were connected by marriage, and analysis of will bequests suggests that they saw themselves as an elite who even lent each other money. The social origins of the majority may have been low, but a significant number were beginning to be drawn from the ranks of the gentry. The status of a clergyman had undoubtedly risen, even though the financial rewards of the job remained poor. A reasonable career ladder existed for bright and well-linked graduates, dependent though this remained on an uncertain patronage system.

There is broad agreement about many of these changes, but not on how they should be interpreted. For Rosemary O'Day they constituted a major breakthrough as the clergy emerged from a medieval 'estate' into an early modern 'profession' (**100**). Central to her argument is the fact that the number of graduates amongst the clergy rose from fairly negligible proportions in the 1570s to almost complete supremacy amongst new ordinands* after the 1620s. In what was partly a cause, but also an effect of this process, the priesthood ceased to be regarded as an office, and became increasingly seen as a pastoral vocation. The clergy, which before the Reformation had consisted of a rather amorphous collection of priests, friars, monks, nuns, and others, became a more united band whose major function was the ministry of the word and service to the community, chiefly through preaching – hence the need for educational qualifications.

This interpretation has not gone unchallenged. It is difficult to sustain claims about 'professionalisation' which have all the hallmarks of twentieth-century preoccupations. The sources for the topic are poor, consisting largely of details of education, ordinations, and clerical appointments. Some of the arguments concerning the rise of a clerical profession, and an attendant degree of 'alienation', seem a little far-fetched for the period. Regional variations were huge, and too much of O'Day's study rests on the declining and poorly documented diocese of Lichfield and Coventry. An apparent improvement in educational qualifications of the clergy seems fairly self-evident, if not the strongest card in this case. Yet Ian Green has warned, 'ministers were in general better educated, but not necessarily better trained for their work' (**155**, p. 285). How far does Rosemary O'Day's case rest on an 'optical illusion' created simply by the fact that graduates came to dominate the ranks of the clergy during this period?

'Professionalisation' may be a red herring, but the changes still call for close scrutiny and interpretation. New demands were clearly being made of the clergy after the Reformation. The Crown, for example, required clergymen to read homilies extolling the virtues of family life and obedience to the state [**doc. 24**]. While many Protestants sought a preaching ministry, others, like Henry Hammond, adopted a wider perspective. Bancroft had occasion to mention prayers, the administration of the sacraments, and the granting of absolution at the Hampton Court Conference*, which Barlow claimed King James 'liked exceeding well, very acutely taxing the hypocrisy of our times which placeth all religion in the ear' (**38**, p. 65). It is important to remember, however, that the clergy did not live in isolation. Not all parishioners welcomed a heightened sense of religious awareness and conscience on the part of their ministers. Catholics preferred to be left alone, and the same is true of the 'reprobates'* who may have had their own 'popular' notions of religion, if they cared at all (**158**).

Key changes for the clergy over the period

First, it is agreed that there was a welcome improvement in the educational qualifications of the clergy over this period. In the 1570s many dioceses like Lincoln, Lichfield & Coventry, and Chester had only a small proportion of graduate clergy. The figure was only one-fifth at Lincoln and still barely a quarter at Lichfield & Coventry even by 1603. Rosemary O'Day claimed that, 'if we turn from this generally dismal state of affairs to the situation in the 1620s, we find that by then recruitment into the Church at parish level is overwhelmingly graduate' (**100**, p. 3). Recent research has shown this to be an exaggeration, but although the south of England fared better than the north, it is still true to say that, overall, very real improvements had been made by 1640 (**58, 168**).

The improvements achieved were a direct consequence of what some historians have described as an 'educational revolution', itself a result of both the spread of Renaissance Humanism and also of the Reformation. Europe at large witnessed a massive expansion in the number of schools and university colleges in the late sixteenth century (**81**). Oxford and Cambridge graduated about 150 students per annum each in 1500; by 1600 that figure stood at 400–500. Jesus College, Oxford, was founded in 1571; Edinburgh gained its university in 1582; the Puritan foundations of Emmanuel College and Sidney Sussex, Cambridge, were laid in 1584 and 1596 respectively. Trinity College, Dublin, was established in 1592. The colleges catered for the gentry and would-be lawyers, but the university curriculum had changed little and was aimed largely at potential clergymen. The Church still provided the best career prospects for able children from humble backgrounds, and richer Protestants felt it was their Christian duty to ensure that those children, along with their own, were well educated. Progress in the establishment of schools to feed these colleges was not just a feature of the famous years of Edward VI's grammar schools. Nor, interestingly, was it peculiarly related to Protestantism; county studies have revealed that Catholic schools were also springing up near market towns, even though they lacked official blessing.

The early Elizabethan Church was staffed by a large number of poorly qualified clergymen, which was a source of great concern to Archbishop Parker, his successor Grindal, and to all godly Puritans*. The vital need to gain a suitably qualified preaching ministry dominated discussions in the late sixteenth century. Initially, many members of the ecclesiastical hierarchy were fully engrossed with this problem. Grindal fell from grace because of his support for the prophesying* movement, which was really, at one level, just a way of carrying out 'in-service training' of the ministry. Others, like Bishop Curteys of Chichester, influenced laymen in the use of their advowsons*, and showed great concern over ordinations. All grappled alike with the vagaries of the patronage system and the problem of how to attract graduates to poorly endowed livings. In 1585 Archbishop Whitgift lamented that there were fewer than 600 livings in total which were capable of supporting a learned minister (**70**).

Puritans* carried out major surveys in the late sixteenth century designed largely to embarrass the authorities over lack of progress in gaining an educated ministry. The two most famous were carried out in 1584–85 and in 1603 – the latter as part of the campaign leading up to the Hampton Court Conference*. Pluralities*, non-resident clergymen and scant preaching were the dominant concerns, along with the detection of scandalous clergymen. A typical entry for the diocese of Chichester in 1603 complained that:

> the number of churches in their country is about 300, of which the impropriations* are 108. The insufficient maintenances are many, and of them 23 not above £16 by the year, and some of £4 or £5. Double beneficed men about 50. Single and yet

non-resident 6. Non preaching 100. Negligent in preaching about 60. Of all these many are scandalous for corrupt life or doctrine. (**149**, p. 188)

The reports were no doubt exaggerated, but Whitgift and his fellow bishops showed that they were well aware of the situation by their own repeated attempts to tighten regulations through Convocation*. They were also under constant pressure from Parliament, and it was this which prompted Whitgift, for instance, when he presented six orders to Convocation in 1589 [**doc. 18**].

Recent research on the Hampton Court Conference* has shed important light on these issues. It is a revealing comment on the lack of progress which had been made by 1603 that the issue of clerical standards figured high on the conference agenda. Although James was once deemed by historians to have swiftly lost interest when this conference closed, he did, in fact, take a very close look at what was going on in East Anglia, encouraging local bishops to take action (**180**). There were other important diocesan dimensions to the aftermath of the conference. Bishops in a number of dioceses, notably Chichester, implemented in-service training programmes for their clergy, possibly because they had been embarrassed by the recent Puritan* surveys, but also because the recent debates did influence many of the new Canons* (**144**). It is ironic how similar these programmes look to the 'exercises'* which had been suppressed under Elizabeth.

When talking about the need for more educated clergy at the conference, James had reflected wisely that 'Jerusalem could not be built up in a day' (**38**, p. 64). Yet the quality of the clergy *was* slowly improving, and as it did so the attitude of the authorities to criticism hardened considerably. After 1603 the issue was really a dead letter, and perhaps what should have worried Puritans* more was that new generations of graduates did not necessarily share the view that the prime role of ministers was to preach. Graduates of the 1590s had come under new influences, and besides, it is possible that their very education in some measure set them apart from their congregations. This argument should not be taken too far because the majority of graduates still went home to find work, largely because of local contacts and the patronage system. High-flying clergymen who came to form the establishment of the Church of England, on the other hand, were by definition highly mobile and developed a strong sense of their *own* community. Maybe a sense of intellectual cameraderie should be added to what we know of the tightly knit 'factions' based on Lambeth Palace and Durham House.

The significance of change – a revitalised clerical estate?

For Rosemary O'Day, the clergy did become a more tightly defined community, largely because so many minor orders* dropped away at the Reformation, leaving membership of the clerical estate more precisely defined. A common educational experience must have added to this sense of *esprit de corps*, though it has to be remembered that the experience was shared with many godly (and not so godly) gentlemen (**100**). Indeed, the 'educational revolution' must have played its part in fuelling rising lay expectations of the clergy, just as much as it gave the latter a greater sense of their own dignity and worth. If one is to judge by the many petitions presented against clergymen in the Long Parliament, many laymen, when confronted by the liturgical* changes introduced by some clergy in the 1630s, came to believe that they, rather than the clerical establishment, had a better understanding of true religion (**107, 131, 147**).

But what is noticeable after 1603 is that it was the clergy who came out fighting for their cause. One of the achievements of Richard Bancroft is that he managed to outmanoeuvre Presbyterian* and Puritan* critics in the late sixteenth century and to steal their clothes. Peter Lake has argued convincingly that the real clericalists of the sixteenth century were the Presbyterians, with their demands that Church and society should be remodelled along the lines adopted at Geneva (**84, 85**). By careful propaganda, Bancroft marginalised this group of critics by tainting them with seeking 'popularity' (which always carried seditious connotations), accusing them of selling out to the laity, and therefore of caring little for the material needs of the Church (**167**). No sooner had *jure divino* claims been successfully staked for episcopacy* than divines like Lancelot Andrewes and George Carleton – from very different wings of the Church – applied similar claims to clerical rights to tithes*. George Carleton's *Tithes Examined and Proved to be due to the Clergy by Divine Right* was published in 1606 and dedicated to Bancroft. It marked the start of a campaign on this issue which affected ecclesiastical policy for the rest of the period. When John Selden published his major work on the subject in 1618, and took a carefully ambivalent position on the origin of tithes, he was savaged by critics including

Richard Montagu, and forced to explain himself personally to the King.

It has already been noted that James I gave his senior clergymen great encouragement by receiving more of them at Court and by appointing several to his Privy Council. Thus assured of royal support, clergymen of all ranks became more assertive. An increased confidence has been detected in the tone of assize sermons printed after 1616. Apparently, clerics were using such occasions to promote their own claims for more secular power. One preacher suggested that if the King wanted harmonious parliaments, he only had to turn to the clergy to tune the pulpits. Attention has already been drawn to the appearance of ordinary clergymen on Commissions of the Peace*. The number of those appointed grew steadily after 1603, and they proved to be assid-uous in their attendance at county Quarter Sessions. And these developments were popular with all factions in the Church. The prominent Calvinist John Davenant felt it was 'no less expedient that clergymen should inflict one kind of chastisement than another' (**1**, p. 49).

Needless to say, these developments started to arouse lay fears even amongst those who had not shared an anti-clerical outlook before. Bills were presented in Parliament regularly in the 1620s in an effort to stop those below the rank of dean from serving on Commissions of the Peace*, and it is all too often forgotten that one of the first acts of the Long Parliament was to forbid this practice. Many members of Parliament felt that the trend for clergymen to exercise secular power was as dangerous as the fact that they also happened to be largely Arminians* by the 1630s. The anti-parliamentarian attitudes of Neile and Laud were well known by the 1640s, but even this trend can be dated back to the begin-ning of the century. John Howson was in trouble in 1604 on account of some 'speeches of scandal and scorn' about the House of Commons; similar cases cropped up in most parliaments there-after, becoming particularly noticeable in the 1620s, when clergymen wrote eagerly in defence of the royal prerogative and the King's right to collect taxes (**114**). Inside Parliament, too, Bancroft was notorious for speaking his mind about those who presented Bills with a 'great deal of spleen against the clergy' (**14**, vol. II, p. 71). And Bishop Neile was found guilty of insulting the Commons in 1614.

Education, changing notions of the 'priesthood', and greater use of new liturgical* practices in worship, particularly amongst the Arminians*, played their part in ensuring that many clergymen came to be seen as having strayed from the true path by the 1640s. And, as Anthony Fletcher notes, the 800 petitions 'which flowed into Westminster in November and December 1640 from the localities complaining about non-preaching and scandalous clergy amply justified the preoccupation of MPs with clerical inadequacy' (**147**, p. 281). Doctrine did indeed play a part in arousing fears, particularly after 1625, but this should not blind us to the full range of secular matters on which clergymen of *all* descriptions found themselves growing steadily at odds with the laity throughout this period. And the trend dates back to 1603 rather than 1625.

In a major article on the clergy, Ian Green pointed to an intriguing paradox that 'at a time when the prospects of a successful career in the church were apparently dismal, an increasing number of young men, most of them well qualified and many from backgrounds of moderate wealth, sought to enter the ministry' (**154**, p. 71). The number of sons of clergymen who followed in their father's footsteps apparently quadrupled between 1600 and 1640, while the number of sons of gentry entering the ministry trebled. It was once popular to argue that there were too many graduates chasing too few jobs in the Church at this time, but the present consensus of opinion suggests that frustrations may have been eased by the sheer variety of positions available, not simply in the parishes, but also fellowships, teaching posts, chaplaincies, and lectureships*. If the prospects were not as bad as was once supposed, it might also be true to say that the rising status of the clergy encouraged many to enter the Church. It is even possible that some were attracted by the new notions of the 'priesthood' entailed in Arminian* views of worship, for it has been pointed out that 'Puritan evangelism was no irresistible force' and that relations between Puritan ministers and their congregations were often strained (**158**).

Economic hardships still accompanied the life of a clergyman, despite the best efforts of Bancroft and later Laud to tackle the problems. Campaigns were launched periodically to regain impropriations*, glebe land*, and tithes* from lay hands, but it is difficult to tell with what real success. Yet bad though the situation may have been for clergy in towns and the poorer livings, it does now look as if a significant number of clergymen managed to do more than make ends meet in the early seventeenth century. But we should not assume that financial considerations were uppermost in the minds of those entering the ministry. Clergymen of all theological shades would no doubt have placed a sense of vocation over their material needs.

Even a sense of vocation could, however, come to be seen in different ways. In the 1630s, Arminian* bishops like Neile and Laud scrutinised graduates carefully, and it was no longer enough to talk of preaching skills and the need for further reformation. Lectureships* were strictly controlled; preaching licences were given sparingly; and the number of ordinations dropped markedly in certain dioceses. Matters probably changed very little over the period for most clergy, who after all had an average span of over fifteen years in any post, a significant number serving livings for over thirty years. New ordinands*, however, were slowly bringing to the Church better educational qualifications, possibly new theological influences, possibly new aspirations and ideals about the nature of the priesthood, providing it with a core of clergy who felt deeply committed to the Church of England, its forms and rituals. Their practical work mirrored the intellectual effort of Hooker in finally establishing the Church of England. Within this achievement, however, may have lain the seeds for the downfall of that Church in the 1640s, as the clergy went too far in their efforts to form once again a significant clerical estate in the land.

6 Church and People

In a rash moment, one historian who should have known better wrote that all our early modern ancestors were 'literal Christian believers' (**86**, p. 74). Heaven only knows how he could tell! Historians can only make educated guesses as to the nature of Christian experience for most people during this period. We may know a little about the views of the 'elite', but the concept of 'popular religion' is beset with difficulties (**48, 181**). It can imply conflict between separate 'elite' and 'popular' cultures, be taken to mean some sort of watered-down version of the official form, or indeed, some legacy of a past set of beliefs which 'coexisted' with a new religion. The topic, in short, is bedevilled with theoretical problems: should we think of 'filter-down' models, 'conflict', 'alternative', or various shades of 'coexistence'? How can we make sense of what most people may have believed at this time?

It is relatively easy to say what was *expected* of most people; namely, that they all should be members of the established Church of England. And in that one statement it becomes obvious that there were problems in practice; Catholic recusants* formed a sizeable minority of the population throughout this period (**40, 41**). A glance at any set of Church court records of the time would pose yet more doubts about the extent of religious conformity. What, for example, does one make of this case from Treyford with Didling in Sussex in 1623, when Richard Knowles was presented*

> for using unreverent speeches by [*sic*] our minister, in disgracing his function and doctrine by his lewd and unreverent speeches, and openly in our hearing in the church before the greater number of the parish saying that his sermon was of nothing but a dead hog, to the great discouraging of our minister to discharge his duties (**25**, p. 64)?

And this was no isolated example of anti-clericalism. Thomas Greene was heard to 'rail bitterly upon our minister' at Felpham in 1622, the same year that Joan Len referred to the incumbent of nearby Littlehampton as 'a lousy minister'. Were these people Catholic recusants*, Puritans*, atheists, people with a personal grudge, or merely drunk (**25**, pp. 33, 49)?

We are doubtful about the notion of 'religious conformity' for a host of reasons. It seems unlikely that the Protestant Reformation can have been entirely successful by the late sixteenth century, even when one discounts the die-hard Catholics. Court records suggest that not only were ministers attacked, sometimes physically, but that a significant number of people were prepared to miss Church services regularly, even upon pain of prosecution. At any one time, maybe as much as 15 per cent of the population were technically excommunicate*, labouring under the most severe penalty the Church could muster – namely, denial of all Christian rights (**93, 94**). Such penalties would have had the greatest effect on a rich man hoping to leave property in a will and to be buried with proper ceremony with a monument, perhaps, in his parish church. It is less easy to imagine how the lower orders might have felt; Church strictures probably had little impact on the poor and the vagrant.

There is evidence that many in society drew comfort from old superstitions and rituals, which conflicted even with Catholicism (**102, 115**). More research is needed on the geography of religion in this period, for although Protestantism may have made ground in the south by 1603, it is clear that it had not done so well in places like Lancashire. The Lake District and Wales were often referred to by both Puritans* and Arminians* as the 'dark corners of the land', and some of the ceremonies practised there had their origins in pagan rather than Christian festivals. Indeed, rush-bearing was still practised in the Lake District as late as the twentieth century. This festival, nominally celebrating the saint's day of the local church, was often an excuse for riotous behaviour. Many were offended by these practices; hence the presentment* of people at Hornby in 1633 'for bearing rushes on the Sabbath day and prophaning the Sabbath with Morris Dances and great fooleries'.

The Book of Sports*, issued in 1618 and re-issued in 1633, could be seen as an attempt by the authorities to neuter the seditious potential of such activities, by giving them official sanction [**doc. 26**]. Demographic change, the appearance of vagrants and 'masterless men', a rising incidence of illegitimate births, rebellious women – all contributed to a feeling that there was a 'crisis of order' (**71, 120**). The Church was in the front line of 'social control', but as David Underdown has reminded us, 'the authority of the new parish elites was not established without opposition and acrimony' (**120**, p. 28). Puritanism* was one response to social instability, but when its disciplines were flouted it was sometimes best to compromise and leave people to their pastimes. Patrick Collinson has suggested that part of the problem could lie with the existence of an adolescent sub-culture, youngsters kicking over the traces (**64**). Evidence from the Church courts suggests that a large number of younger people were frequently involved in misdemeanours, much as today, and that the Church was scorned as a bastion of authority. An alternative 'ale-house culture' has also been posited, an idea which likewise rings true today!

The Church was in the firing line with regard to enforcing moral and community standards, but its power should not be exaggerated. Significant groups already noted, like the poor, the disreputable, recalcitrant Catholics, and youthful elements, felt relatively immune from its authority and careless of its sanctions. It has been wisely noted that the real division in this early modern society was not between social groups, or the young and the old, but simply between the 'godly' and the 'ungodly' (**47, 48, 49**). Puritans* may have criticised the Church courts, but they wanted their controls as much as any bishop. The Church courts only operated effectively when they had community sanction; they were used by various groups in society in the 'war' against sinfulness, particularly where that involved unwanted pregnancies and costs for the parish. As population pressures rose in the late sixteenth century, so too did prosecutions, as the 'moral majority' took action to maintain its codes of conduct (**78, 79, 127**).

One way of approaching this topic is to ask, fairly crudely, what the Church did for ordinary people. For the religious, it clearly gave them a theology and organised rituals of worship. Disputes about these matters were not confined to the elite members of society, as the explosion of different sects during the 1640s reveals, but it was the educated who defined the battle zones during the period covered by this book. In the parishes, the Church still offered the predominant way of organising knowledge of the world. This is a rich theme mined so wonderfully by Keith Thomas in his *Religion and the Decline of Magic* (**115**). The Reformation destroyed older unified pictures of the world, and the role of the priest as a magician was lost; it is argued that magic, now that it had been freed from religion, gave rise to the witchcraft craze of the late sixteenth and early seventeenth centuries. It is now more appreciated than ever that Protestantism, with its stress on literacy and the word, was not necessarily 'popular'. A harking back to pre-Reformation security is a theme which crops up in various parts of this book, for it was clearly a factor for those who remained Catholics, and may have subtly influenced Arminian* interest in old liturgical* practices.

If Protestantism lacked emotional appeal, the Church still provided a framework for life. Church festivals – particularly Christmas and Easter – gave shape to the calendar, and there were always crops to be blessed and harvest festivals (**102, 181**). The Church played a critical role in determining the rites of passage through life, for it registered the major ceremonies of baptism, marriage, and burial. Finally, the Church was a major influence in bonding the community together. One function of the minister was to settle neighbourhood disputes. Community values influenced the nature of the presentments* made to the Church courts; if the 'godly' were in charge, then the Church was used very clearly as a weapon of 'social control' (**79, 109**). At all times, of course, the government ensured that its own power was reinforced: homilies on obedience and the royal supremacy, plus the presence of the royal coat of arms in every parish church, were a constant reminder of secular authority. Church ceremonies often promoted a sense of community in very physical ways, such as the harvest festivals, or perambulation* of parish boundaries in Rogation week. The latter processions were often associated with the provision of food for the poor, and were occasions on which the theme of good neighbourliness was exhorted and given public and practical expression.

It would be erroneous to assume that religion meant the same things to all people. There are many examples of ignorance, atheism, agnosticism, and superstition in the cases brought before the Church courts. For many people there seems to have been no problem about holding several apparently contradictory sets of beliefs. Once the effectiveness of the minister as a general counsellor and wise man had been doubted, as at the Reformation, many people sought alternative sources of advice and thought nothing of attending services to pray for aid and consulting a 'white [that is, good] witch' at the same time (**92**). This should hardly surprise us in our own age of 'alternative medicines' and great interest in astrology. What matters is that the Church still operated at many levels for most people. It was a social centre if nothing else – something complained of by the Arminians* when they found churches being used for court meetings, town gatherings, schools, and even in some cases, markets. For the majority, the church was a centre of religious life, even if it now seems wisest for historians to follow the example set by Queen Elizabeth in being concerned with outward observances rather than worrying too much about inner thoughts.

Grave doubts have been expressed about the impact of Protestantism by 1603, and indeed it seems most unlikely, as Patrick Collinson has pointed out, 'that an intellectually demanding and morally rigorous religion transmitted by the written and spoken word had a broad, natural appeal' (**47**, p. 201). Puritan* evangelists fought a tough battle with the forces of Satan and the world, and the alehouse was a strong adversary, not to mention people's love of popular pastimes, invariably conducted on the Sabbath. The sources from which the historian tries to estimate how successful were the attempts to create a 'godly' nation are notoriously difficult to evaluate, but there are signs that recent pessimism may have been overdone, and they come from unexpected quarters.

It is a commonplace observation that churches fell into physical neglect in the sixteenth century. This led Patrick Collinson to remark that 'whereas it is proper to measure the strength of pre-Reformation sentiment by its material remains, it would be a mistake to gauge the quality of post-Reformation religion by the same criterion' (**134**, p. 171). Yet it now seems that this is precisely one measure that we might use to suggest that Protestantism had taken a hold of the hearts and minds of many in the local communities. Evidence based on studies of churchwardens'* accounts points to a significant rise in expenditure on churches in the Jacobean period, pre-dating the famous campaigns of the 1630s which were heavily concerned with 'beautification' of churches and altar changes. The figures add weight to the recent surmises of Diarmaid MacCulloch that there was a minor 'building revolution' which affected parishes churches beginning at the end of the sixteenth century (**172**). In response to criticisms, Archbishop Whitgift had carried out a survey of churches in 1602, and called for improvements; now it seems that something came of his call. This thought led MacCulloch to speculate further that Neile and Laud aroused hostility in the 1630s, 'not because they were stirring up previously inactive church officers to save tottering and neglected fabrics but precisely because they often interfered with recently completed schemes of refurnishing and restoration' (**172**, p. 14).

Church courts

Like it or not, few people could escape the jurisdiction of the Church in this period. A battery of courts extending from the High Commission* and the Courts of Arches* and Delegates*, through to the ordinary consistory courts of each diocese, had jurisdiction over a broad spectrum of everyday life (**79**). It has already been noted that attendance at church was expected in this society, as indeed was the regular taking of communion. Likewise, the Church controlled the 'rites of passage' referred to earlier. Failure to comply with regulations in these matters usually brought one into contact with the courts. Prerogative courts in every diocese, plus two at provincial level and a variety of appeal courts, determined all probate* business. Only the poor escaped that bureaucratic nightmare. Visitation* courts monitored the work of the clergy and checked on general obedience to the Canons*. Visitations were a constant feature of life, for they could occur twice a year at archidiaconal level, at least once every three years in the case of most bishops, and could even be held on a provincial basis, as was the case when Archbishops Neile and Laud held their notorious metropolitical visitations in the 1630s [**docs 22** and **23**].

This picture of an awesome battery of courts must be softened by an awareness that theory was seldom matched by practice. Compliance with the Church courts was a problem throughout this period, and as has been mentioned earlier, problems grew for the authorities as they went down the social scale and also as they travelled in the more remote regions. The Church courts were heavily dependent on the goodwill and integrity of locally elected churchwardens*. Such people could easily be intimidated, and it was rare for a churchwarden to present* a social superior, whatever the crime. Viscount Montague of Midhurst, one of the south's most prominent Catholics, was only presented by churchwardens during the war years of the 1620s. Church lay officials were invariably drawn from local families and granted their jobs for life; as a consequence, it could prove extremely difficult for a bishop to remove a corrupt administrator.

So far we have been dealing with the courts in their official, disciplinary capacities. However, a large part of the business of the consistory courts* was taken up with 'instance' cases, which were brought by individuals against other individuals, and in which evidence would be heard on both sides. It is thanks largely to research on this aspect of the Church courts that they have

59

emerged from a predominantly bad press over recent years. It was relatively easy to find evidence in literature and parliamentary debates of this period that Church courts were detested by common lawyers, and were frequently accused of corrupt practices, outmoded rules, excessive fees, and protracted proceedings (**71**). Much of the flak was directed against the prerogative court of High Commission*, which had unique powers to imprison, but which ironically contained many laymen as judges, and had originally been established to root out Catholic recusants*. It was this court which played such an unpopular role in the persecution of critics of the regime in the 1630s that it was swiftly abolished by the Long Parliament in 1641 (**121**). Its powers to imprison and exact large fines seem to have been used against people from all social classes – as, for instance, when Sir Pexal Brocus was forced to do penance clad only in a white sheet in St Paul's in 1613. Yet the role of the High Commission has been allowed to cast too big a shadow over the work of the rest of the Church courts. Its influence may even have been exaggerated, for in the 1630s it was closely linked in both personnel and policy with the prerogative court of Star Chamber (**179**). It was also used by the government as an instrument for the advancement of censorship laws.

But to return to the Church courts in general, there are several strands in the debate on their role which have shed new light on their function and utility in society. Ecclesiastical historians like Ronald Marchant, Jean Potter, and Ralph Houlbrooke have tested, and found wanting, old assumptions about the inefficiency, corruption, and decline of the Church courts (**82, 93, 94, 109**). As Marchant proclaimed:

> The church courts and their officers are too often seen through the eyes of Puritan* and legal propagandists as the outworn relics of the Papal system. They were rather in a flourishing condition, and representative of a vigorous legal tradition. (**93**, p. 1)

The Church courts were indeed threatened by the impact of the Reformation, and then by Puritans*, yet they survived to perform quite well in the late sixteenth century and indeed to undergo a revival in the 1620s and 30s under the spur of the Arminians*.

They survived not only because they were useful to an ecclesiastical hierarchy increasingly concerned with maintaining order, but because they also served a useful social function in the community at large. They were part of what one historian has described as the transition from a violent, feudal age to 'civil society'. Here the work of Martin Ingram and Jim Sharpe has been very informative: they have drawn heavily on anthropology and sociology to show that the courts were particularly useful in the late sixteenth century as the country experienced quite rapid population growth. The courts acted as a 'safety valve' through which local communities could exercise social control. They were frequently used to enforce oaths and promises, to defend the 'honour' of people slighted, to ratify marriage contracts, and to apportion responsibility in bastardy cases so as to limit the burdens which could otherwise be placed on parish poor relief (**79, 109, 120, 163**). Half of the business of the Chester courts was concerned with the regulation of personal conduct; fornication invariably represented 30 per cent of the visitation* case load, and 43 per cent of all instance cases were to do with slander and defamation. Overall, the work of the Chester courts doubled between 1544 and 1594 (defamation cases quadrupled within that figure) (**109**).

Historians working at a parish level have also confirmed just how concerned the local elites in any community were to maintain their position in the face of very unsettled times, most notably in the 1590s when harvests failed several years running (**78, 127, 189**). The issue is extremely complicated, however, for the rise in reported sexual offences could also have been a by-product of the increased pressure placed on the Church courts by the authorities. It may well be that at times when the authorities called for action against nonconformity, churchwardens* obliged by presenting more offenders, but not of the type required.

While it is possible to show that the Church courts were more effective than once thought, older images do still have some value, for they represent what many people *felt* about these courts. The number of visitation* presentments* in the diocese of York in 1633 was 140 per cent up on 1595, and a relatively creditable 66 per cent of those presented obeyed the summons to appear (**93**). But such efficiency can scarcely have been popular. Clashes with the common-law courts occurred in 1606 and again in 1611, when Abbot successfully defended the Church against writs of prohibition, whereby cases were switched to secular courts. Parliamentary evidence suggests that the Church courts were a constant cause of complaint; there were Bills on the subject in practically every Parliament. In 1614 Sir Maurice Berkeley alleged that Church courts were 'more charge to the subject than 4 subsidies'. In the corruption scandals of 1621, four Bills concerned Church courts and issues like fees, impartiality, fines, and commutations of penances. No fewer than seven of the seventeen new Canons* of 1640 were directed at reforming acknowledged abuses – for example, 'vexatious citations' (**7, 71, 104, 114, 136**).

Several of the new Canons* concerned the role of court officials, notably the chancellors of dioceses. In 1621 Sir John Lambe, Sir John Bennet, and John Craddock, all leading officials of different dioceses, were indicted on various charges of corruption (**87, 104**). Chancellors were very powerful figures in any diocese, for they were the chief legal advisers to the bishops. But there was more here than concern over individuals. The system itself was under attack. Research on civil lawyers* as a group indicates that they were naturally predisposed to be loyal and obedient servants of the Crown and Church. Often from humble backgrounds, the 200-odd civil lawyers of the country represented a maligned but hard-working segment of the legal profession (**87**). They were tainted with the charge of Popery because they operated Roman law*, and their numbers were declining, so it is little wonder that they clung to the authorities who still supported them. One of their number was Dr John Cowell, whose law dictionary, *The Interpreter*, was condemned in Parliament in 1610 for according the King absolute power. This same Dr Cowell worked closely with Bancroft, Lambe, and Neile over the campaign for greater clerical conformity initiated in 1604 (**87**).

One characteristic of the Arminians* was the way in which they praised the attitude of civil lawyers* and cultivated contacts through their meeting place at Doctors' Commons. Laud, Andrewes, Harsnett, Neile, and Juxon were all honorary members of that society. Neile in particular had close ties with civil lawyers and actually had a hand in training William Easdall in the profession (**148**). Easdall started his career as a legal secretary to Neile at Westminster and moved with him to Rochester, Lichfield & Coventry, and Lincoln. Easdall became Chancellor of Durham diocese late in Neile's career there, but was at York when Neile was appointed Archbishop in 1633. He was godfather to Neile's grandchild. It was Easdall who supervised Neile's primary visitation* of York province, enabling the latter to stay in London and attend important Privy Council meetings (**93**). It was that kind of thing which was complained of so often in Parliament. Canon twelve of 1640 firmly curtailed the practice of lay Chancellors censuring clergy.

Arminians* seem to have appreciated that in order to hold power effectively they needed to control not only the top ecclesiastical posts in the land, but also the administrative bureaucracy of the Church. They had targeted the masterships of Oxford and Cambridge colleges successfully in the early 1600s. Subsequently, they exerted their influence on appointments to legal positions in diocesan administration. They never gained complete control, of course, but their tactics received the backhanded compliment of a bitter attack by William Prynne, as has already been noted (see pp. 29–32). Events in the 1630s added many new charges to those which were traditionally levelled at the Church courts. They were accused of being used in a partisan manner to gag 'godly' clergymen and to enforce new liturgical* practices. It is indeed the case that the nature of 'crimes' expanded greatly over the period. It was one thing to urge the removal of the altar to the east end, but it was another to request the taking of communion at the rail, which was not required by any Canon*. The Canons of 1640 apparently confirmed what many critics of the establishment had been claiming – namely, that 'the definition of 'Puritan'* had been extended to include all who opposed any aspect of current orthodoxy in the Church of England [**docs. 26** and **27**].

It is possible to exonerate the Church courts from some of the charges levelled against them in this period. They do seem to have fulfilled a useful social function, particularly concerning the supervision of codes of conduct. Although there were corrupt individuals, the system functioned relatively well, and indeed business increased over the period. The events of the 1630s placed a great strain on goodwill, however, and re-activated fears of Popery. It was hardly surprising that these 'Roman' courts were swept away during the Interregnum, and although they returned with the Restoration they never regained anything like their former jurisdiction. Puritans* of the 1570s had complained because they lacked control of the Church courts and could not therefore use them as a weapon in their fight against a sinful world. Many Puritans of the 1630s fled the country when they discovered that the courts were being revitalised, but only so that they could be used against them in the fight to impose order and uniformity on the Church of England.

7 The Church in the 1630s

This decade has always been seen as critical in the history of the Church (**50**). It embraces the 'personal rule' or 'eleven years' tyranny' from 1629 to 1640, when Archbishop William Laud appeared to reign supreme in both Church and state. In 1632 his old patron Richard Neile became Archbishop of York, and his new-found ally Thomas Wentworth, later Earl of Strafford, became Lord Deputy of Ireland. Although Laud became Archbishop of Canterbury only in 1633, he had been effectively in charge of the Church since at least 1627. In 1636 his friend William Juxon, Bishop of London, became the first clergyman since the reign of Henry VII to hold the post of Lord Treasurer. Little wonder, then, that William Laud was seen as one of the architects of the Civil War; his policies created a stir in England, while his attempts to introduce changes in Scotland led to the so-called 'Bishops' Wars' after 1638. Given that these led inexorably to the Long Parliament of 1640, the case against Laud looks strong. And indeed, Laud paid the ultimate price of his own life when convicted on such charges by contemporaries in 1645.

So what exactly happened in the 1630s to arouse such passions? Surely the period simply witnessed a continuation of the policies already being pursued in some dioceses like Durham, Winchester, and Norwich in the 1620s? That is true, but the question is loaded. The personalities and events of the 1630s are open to many inter-pretations. For Peter Heylyn, Laud's chaplain and biographer, the Archbishop was simply trying to bring order and decency to worship in England (**21**). For William Prynne, on the other hand, Laud was akin to Antichrist himself, engaged in an attempt to drag the Church of England back to Rome (**32, 33**). Moderates caught in the middle, like Edward Hyde, later Earl of Clarendon, admired Laud's energy and commitment, yet also felt embarrassed by his brusque manner. Whatever one concludes about the nature of the policies, the cartoons of people like Thomas Stirry reveal widespread hatred for Laud and many of his bishops by the 1640s [**doc. 28**].

Just as contemporaries took up extreme positions about Laud's aims, methods, and possible ambitions, so too historians have differed dramatically in their interpretation of events in the 1630s. For Nicholas Tyacke and historians who employ the concept of Arminianism*, this period witnessed the complete seizure of power by the Arminians and the full implementation of policies nurtured in only one or two dioceses in earlier decades. The stress placed on liturgical* changes, they argue, was perfectly logical given Arminian views on worship and the role of the 'priesthood' (**118, 148, 150**). Other historians, while conceding that major changes took place in the 1630s, prefer to characterise events under the more theologically neutral label of 'Laudianism', even though this is essentially an historians' concept rather than one used widely by contemporaries (**70, 74, 126**). They take at face value the denials of Laud, Neile, and others that they were Arminians, regardless of the political circumstances in which these statements were invariably made, and tend to emphasise discrete policies such as the search for uniformity, concern for the economic plight of the Church, and support for royal absolutism (**117, 185, 193, 194, 126**). This approach removes any real theological justification for the policies pursued, and defines Laud as basically a conservative theologian and administrator, who hankered after greater order and decency for its own sake. According to Christopher Hill, 'Laudianism then was a policy rather than a theology' and one which owed much to the tradition established by Whitgift and Bancroft (**74**, p. 75).

More recently, as a tide of 'revisionism' has swept over Stuart studies, we have been asked to be more sympathetic towards Laud. His dreams have been subjected to analysis and apparently there is 'no doubt that both asleep and awake Laud was a very troubled man' (**43**)! We are even urged to consider the possibility that Laud was no theologian at all, but simply an administrator humbly doing the bidding of his royal master (**110, 128, 185**). It is pointed out, quite correctly, just how many orders were signed by the King, as if this really indicates how policy was made. Finally, to add to the confusion, we have been informed that the term 'Laudian' is deeply misleading because Laud himself was far from being the real leader, or most effective member, of his 'party' on many issues which have since become regarded as hallmarks of policy in this era, such as the campaign to restore altars to the east end of churches (**54**). This attack does more damage to those who prefer the label of 'Laudianism' than it does to those who talk of

'Arminianism'*, for it has often been noted that younger Arminians, like William Piers and Matthew Wren, were more outspoken, more aggressive, and more inflexible in pursuit of policies, than their elders like Neile, Laud, and Buckeridge.

Some historians still prefer to see the Puritans* as the trouble-makers of the period and reject Tyacke's claims that they were pushed into action by an Arminian* take-over of the Church of England (**194**). In their view, if Puritans were harshly dealt with in the 1630s, they only got what they deserved. Taking this approach a stage further, it has even been suggested that Laud's policies may have been quite popular! If one accepts that there was a large constituency of people who still hankered after Catholicism, then the liturgical* changes of the 1630s may have fulfilled a deep-seated need for ritual and ceremony in life (**61**). However, one does not need to go this far to concede that there were moderates in the Church, people like Joseph Hall, James Ussher, and Henry King, who tried to hold out against extremism of all kinds until they too were swept away in the tide of hatred which engulfed the Church in the 1640s.

Some words of warning are necessary before considering key features of the policies pursued in the 1630s (**150**). They may also shed some light on why there is room for so much controversy. First, we have to remember that the pace of implementation of policies differed dramatically from region to region. Even in the 1630s, 'Laudian' or 'Arminian'* bishops did not control all dioceses, and there were shades of opinion and episcopal style within the 'party'; not all were as efficient as Richard Neile and Matthew Wren. On the other hand, the staunch Calvinist Bishop Davenant, the independent John Williams, Bishop of Lincoln, and secret Catholic, Godfrey Goodman, Bishop of Gloucester, were hardly model bishops as far as Laud was concerned. Second, lack of sources for some dioceses distorts our picture of what was achieved. Third, because we know that the programme was cut off dramatically in 1640, it is difficult to evaluate policies which may have been in their infancy. We can detect claims by clergy for secular power, a major programme of ceremonial changes, and considerable support for royal authority, but it is very difficult to know how these policies might have been pursued after 1640 and where they might have led. Finally, it is important to remember that many of the points of controversy stem from the fact that historians choose to select and order the various policies in different ways, and indeed, some would argue that these policies do not in fact have an overall coherence and rationale sufficient to be described as a programme (**54**).

Key policies of the 1630s

Central to the policies pursued in the 1630s was the drive for greater uniformity amongst both clergy and laity. It was so dominant that T.M. Parker concluded in ringing terms that 'it was not so much doctrine as discipline which was the distinguishing mark of the Laudian' (**178**, p. 33). For years the Arminians* had been railing at the Puritan* obsession with preaching as the chief function of the ministry; now they had the chance to emphasise other important concerns like the sacraments, prayer, and the catechism*. Orders of 1629 laid down tight regulations governing the work of lecturers*, seen by Laud as subversive because they were often found in towns, funded and appointed by laypeople, and not subject to episcopal control because they lacked proper benefices*. Where lectureships were allowed to survive, the clergy concerned had to promise to accept benefices when they became available and to subject themselves to normal authority. Pressure was applied to replace afternoon lectures with more easily regulated catechism classes. The rights of gentry to maintain chaplains and private chapels were heavily curtailed. Meanwhile, bishops were ordered to examine ordinands* carefully and to restrict the number of preaching licences they issued. Archbishop Neile took such orders to heart, complained about the lack of good candidates for ordination, and gave licences to preach only to his most trusted clergy – a dramatic reduction on earlier years given the size of his diocese and province (**150**).

The battle for uniformity turned partly on the question of control of livings. A group known as the Feoffees for Impropriations*, based in London, had begun buying up impropriations* and advowsons* in order that they could appoint clergy of their choice and inclinations to the livings concerned (**130**). This smacked of lay control of the Church to Laud, and the Feoffees were ordered to disband in 1633. More positively, friends of Laud, most notably Viscount Scudamore, were persuaded to restore impropriations to the Church, an idealistic scheme once proposed by James I. Meanwhile, the clergy were asked to provide more information on their plight, as a guide to the best way in which to effect material reforms in the parishes. Glebe terriers* were required for the metropolitical visitations*, which also saw an increase in cases presented concerning neglect of Church property. The number of tithe* disputes increased in the 1630s as both clergy and laity became more conscious of Church property rights. Ironically, it seems that lay impropriators were keener than the clergy to insist on these rights, possibly because the clergy were loath to arouse friction with their flock.

At both diocesan and parish level, Laud sought to re-invigorate the Church. Bishops were urged to make regular reports, to keep residence and to carry out property surveys and improvements [**doc. 13**]. Bishop John Bancroft obligingly built a palace for the diocese of Oxford at Cuddesdon, while Neile set in train restoration work on the palaces of York and Southwell (**148**). Old abuses were finally curtailed, like the felling of trees from Church property before they were fully mature and therefore worth the best price. Asset-stripping had not only been the prerogative of Queen Elizabeth and her favourites; bishops, who were increasingly family men, often sought to provide for their children by awarding favourable leases to property. Promotion to a new diocese could mean a rush to push through rather dubious leases before leaving (**70**). It was a common cry of opponents of episcopacy* that bishops, especially those of low social origins, were too concerned with temporal needs at the expense of spiritual. Calls for reform had been made since the time of Elizabeth, but Laud was the first archbishop to take effective action. In 1634 bishops and cathedral chapters were ordered to grant leases for only twenty-one years, instead of, as hitherto, for three lives. Yet the damage had been done, and bishops in the 1630s found it almost impossible to regain control of property which had been granted out on ninety-nine-year leases. Richard Montagu complained in 1634 that eight manors lost in 1561, which would have been worth over £2,500, had been exchanged for impropriations* which brought in a mere £228 (**149**).

One of the most successful campaigns of the 1630s concerned the restoration of churches (**148, 150**). A royal proclamation of 1629 signalled the start of the campaign, particularly in the north, while a commission for the repair of St Paul's Cathedral, subject to sporadic restoration work under James I, symbolised concern in the south after 1631 (**118**). It has already been suggested that these campaigns may simply have given greater government sanction to work which some communities were already undertaking voluntarily after 1603 (**172**). Much was achieved in the 1630s as thousands of pounds were spent on churches throughout the country. Yet what gave this laudable work a sour taste for many was that it became associated with new liturgical* practices involving the placing of communion tables as altars at the east end of churches, with rails for protection. It was this policy more than any other that gave rise to acute fears that Laud was attempting to take the Church of England back to Rome. It was this policy which led to a famous test case when the parishioners of St Gregory's in London took the matter to the Privy Council, where the King decided in favour of the bishops in 1633. Whitgift had inaugurated a major campaign in 1602, James I had shown interest in the plight of St Paul's before, but by the 1630s many of the reforms were tainted with Arminianism* as altars were erected, organs revamped, fonts decorated, elaborate pews cut down, and pulpits marginalised. Such changes were not only theologically anathema to the devout; they were also costly. Indications from surviving accounts suggest that Church rates may have trebled in the 1630s to meet these costs (**150**).

Tighter control of the clergy entailed greater observance of ceremonial in Church services. Ministers found themselves suspended if they failed to wear the surplice*, administer communion only at the altar rail, bow at the name of Jesus, or observe the strict use of the liturgy*. The homilies* and the use of catechism* classes were emphasised in an attempt to limit opportunities for impromptu sermons on taboo subjects. There is no denying that this represented quite a break with the more lax approach of the ecclesiastical authorities towards such matters prior to 1625. Nor is it any wonder that the 1630s saw many ministers depart for Holland and the New World. As George Herbert, the poet and divine, wrote: 'religion stands on tiptoe in our land, ready to pass to the American strand' (**23**, p. 162). Commissions were established to control the colonies in 1634 and 1636, but this was clearly a forlorn, if revealing, hope. The bishops did, however, try to monitor some of the ministers who left the country, and the exodus was viewed with mixed feelings. It was good when troublemakers went into exile, but it also emphasised the extent of the battle still to be won at home. Paranoid reactions were not only the province of Puritans*, for the bishops played constantly on the fears of Charles I that he faced a major 'puritan conspiracy' to take over the Church.

Evidence of these fears can be found in the manner in which the Arminians* punished opponents of their regime, surely one enduring symbol which sparks thoughts of 'tyranny'. The treatment of William Prynne, Henry Burton, and John Bastwick was singularly brutal in the 1630s, but they were not the only 'martyrs' to the cause. Alexander Leighton also suffered for his book *An Appeal to Parliament, or Sion's Plea against the Prelacie*, published in 1628. The elderly Peter Smart was hauled down to prison in London for having spoken out against the changes which had taken place at Durham. Bishop John Williams of Lincoln was 'framed' on trumped-up charges relating to his time as Lord Keeper, partly because he opposed the altar policy. Spies were set to watch notable Calvinist bishops like Thomas Morton of Durham. The tone of this regime is vividly caught in the reports which Sir Nathaniel Brent, Laud's Vicar-General, made during his metropolitical visitation* [**doc. 23**] (**50, 118, 150**).

In this context, the improvement in the machinery and operation of the Church courts – so long called for by Puritans* anxious for control of the forces of Satan – took on a sinister aspect as the 'godly' themselves became targets of ecclesiastical justice. The metropolitical visitations* of Neile and Laud were the most effective and far-reaching in living memory. The whole country was surveyed by Church commissioners led by Sir Nathaniel Brent and William Easdall. The court of High Commission* was active in bringing Puritan ministers to account and in harrying the laity who protected them. It is small wonder that Prynne, Burton, and Bastwick bitterly attacked this court in 1637 and tried to question the authority of episcopal visitations. But there was little point in complaining about the blurring of the line between secular and episcopal authority, for that very ambiguity was working to the advantage of the state. The annual reports of bishops provided new information for the government on life in the regions, while the appointment of clergy as Justices of the Peace ensured the presence of loyal Crown servants in local decision making. Clerical JPs – loyal eyes and ears of the Crown – were seen as doubly desirable in towns, which were regarded as potential centres of sedition. It was significant that the 1630s witnessed moves to renew many cathedral town charters in an effort to increase clerical representation in local government (**150**).

Control was what the Arminians* sought so keenly, and over many aspects of life. Schools and universities found themselves inspected by the bishops; subscription to the Three Articles [**doc. 7**] was required of teachers as well as clergy. New Oxford statutes were issued in 1636 which showed Laud's tidy mind at work in reforming abuses and laying down high standards of practice (**186**). Control of the presses was also sought, even if rarely fully achieved. In this early modern society it was impossible to stop the publication of books and pamphlets, which were often printed abroad and smuggled into England to get around the licensing controls established in 1626 and tightened by a Star Chamber decree of 1637. It is easy for us to note how ineffective these early controls were, but the explosion of publications when the censorship was raised in the 1640s reveals that they must have had some effect. Moreover, it was the intention – and how it was perceived – that matters, expecially when placed in context with other events in the 1630s (**58, 132, 143, 162**).

During the 1630s many people came to believe that the clergy had lost sight of their original preaching function and concern for peace in the community, and were more interested in prosecuting 'godly' people for trivial breaches of ceremonial, depriving them of sermons, allowing abuse of the Sabbath day, and supporting the King no matter what levies he chose to raise, like Ship Money or forced loans. There were howls of anguish and many suspensions of clergy when the Book of Sports*, which permitted recreations on the Sabbath, was re-issued in 1633 [**doc. 25**]. Francis White's treatise on the issue in 1635 did little but inflame matters further. The Church was becoming steadily entangled with affairs of state – so much so that even where its religious policies may have been given the benefit of the doubt, its relationship with the state aroused fears. Juxon's appointment as Lord Treasurer in 1636 reminded people of Cardinal Wolsey. Bishops on the Privy Council, sitting in Star Chamber, acting on Commissions for the Poor Law, the presence of clerical Justices of the Peace on county benches – all smacked of an unacceptable resurgence of clerical power. This explains some of the violent feelings voiced in the Root and Branch petitions of 1640 [**doc. 27**]. The definition of 'scandalous clergy' now included Arminians* and royal time-servers.

Laud and his colleagues overreached themselves in the 1630s. They tried to do too much, too quickly, and in too many countries. It was one thing to get new Canons* passed in the Irish Convocation of 1634, when Wentworth maintained a strong grip on that land; it was quite another to get the Scots to accept a new Prayer Book in 1636. Laud and his colleagues breathed new life into the Church bureaucracy of the time, and felt doubly secure that they had the ear of the King, but they alienated a significant number of English people and gave substance to fears of a

Catholic plot (**67**). They were not helped by the fact that there was a spate of Court converts to Catholicism in this period, or by the activities of papal envoys like Gregorio Panzani and George Conn who fanned fears of the role of the Queen.

In the final analysis, it hardly matters what label historians employ to describe these events, nor whether it will ever be possible to say with certainty who really initiated the policies. Contemporaries had little doubt that the cause of their problems lay with Arminianism*. What to them had started as a movement 'to usher in Popery' had become even more obviously part of a Popish conspiracy by the 1640s; hence the rhetoric which prevailed in the Long Parliament. Arminian beliefs in the sacraments and worship gave the policies of the 1630s intellectual coherence, but in popular mythology it was just as likely to be the Arminian association with increased claims for the clergy, or connections with secular power, or the visible impact and cost of ceremonial changes which caused offence. Matters had gone far beyond the niceties of doctrines of predestination* which so upset members of the intellectual elite. The physical removal of a communion table to the east end of a church, to be renamed an altar and railed in, carried enormous symbolic and material connotations. Educated Puritans* took offence at the implied theology of the changes, gentry were outraged when their pews were cut down to size, parishioners were upset by the increased costs of restoring and maintaining the fabric of their churches, and many would have noticed that they were now in a different relationship with their minister. Laud's vision of Church and society may have been fair and ordered; it may have appealed to more than hitherto supposed, and worked in the interests of social justice; but such considerations cut little ice with members of Parliament when retribution for the policies of the 1630s was sought after 1640.

Part Three: Assessment

8 Changing Perspectives on the Church of England

It is natural that our perspective on the Church should change over time. New evidence materialises, new questions are posed, new approaches are adopted, and we need to keep reviewing common assumptions and traditional ways of thinking. It is vital to monitor the many ways in which altered perceptions of people, events, critical dates, and concepts shift and affect our whole outlook on a period and topic. We have seen how views of the relative merits of Elizabeth I, James I, and Charles I have changed in recent times. Hence we now look upon Elizabeth's contribution to the Church of England in less rosy terms than hitherto, see James in a more sympathetic and rational light, and despair about the political wisdom of Charles I. Likewise, many scholars now write fondly of Archbishops Grindal and Abbot, as moderate Calvinists who sought to maintain a broad Church. While some acknowledge the practical achievements of Whitgift and Bancroft, most still generally feel that something went badly wrong under William Laud.

Interest in the nature of Puritanism, Catholicism, and economic problems of the Church has given way to greater emphasis on the very *structure* of the Church, its clergy, its courts, its bishops, and the way it functioned in society prior to the Civil War. We are dealing with a very complex institution, and we need to see the Church from many angles in order to appreciate how it worked for all people rather than just the political elite. Our agenda has become more complicated, as Patrick Collinson acknowledged when he wrote that

The task of the religious historian of England between the Elizabethan Settlement and the Civil War is thus one of daunting complexity.... Somehow he must describe two almost antithetical processes: on the one hand, the emergence of a growing diversity in religious culture, on the other, the simultaneous adoption by a major section of the nation of a consensual Protestantism closely connected to a sense of national identity and to principles of civil obedience and deference, edged with a frank hostility for Catholic foreign powers and for the Pope himself. (**134,** p. 175)

Much of this book has been concerned with the attempts of the authorities to control and stabilise the Church; it is never as easy to do full justice to the many tensions at work within a changing 'religious society'.

Puritanism* will always attract research, partly because Americans are so interested in their origins, but even here the emphasis has changed to give us a better awareness of what motivated Puritans and what they feared. We recognise their obsession with Antichrist and can see how this affected their desire to lead simple, godly lives free from wordly temptations: drink, ribaldry, and sexual licence. It is good, however, that we no longer see them as the dominant group in society, the only ones who sought to impose their religious values on others. We have become aware of the destabilising role of Arminian* theologians, but also conscious of other voices which still require more attention from historians [**doc. 19**]. There were many competing groups in the Church, each with broadly similar aims concerning the need to reform society. The irony has often been noted that Archbishop Laud was as obsessed with the need for order and uniformity as any godly Puritan, and the measures undertaken by Puritans to regulate society during the Interregnum were no more successful than his in the 1630s.

The Church was a constantly evolving institution over this period. The rescue of the useful concept of Arminianism* from obscurity has helped to re-focus attention. It has highlighted the importance of events in Cambridge in the 1590s and at the Court of James I in the early 1600s, and has confirmed the significance of radical innovations after 1625. Our greater knowledge of the factional politics of the Courts of the early Stuarts has likewise helped our understanding of the ways in which one Church faction came to destabilise an entire state. When considering important dates, however, there is still great debate as to the relative significance of 1603 and 1625 as critical 'turning-points'. The latter date is most fashionable, partly because it suits 'revisionist' thinking, but also because it marks the point at which Arminians finally gained power. It is the contention of this book, however, that many important trends need to be taken back to the accession of James I. It was in the years after 1603 that Arminians became visible in Court politics and that the clerical estate began its resurgence.

Fears, preoccupations, and different Church groups

Whilst theological doctrine is important, we need to remember the *emotional* impact of the Church. Doctrine may have preoccupied the thoughts of the elite, but religious faith and fears affected all levels of society. Mention of Antichrist makes one aware of the belief of Puritans that the devil constantly walked the land. From this perspective we can understand their concern about the introduction of greater ceremonial in the 1620s and '30s. Allied to their fears was an exaggerated 'respect' and awe of things Catholic, particularly where the Jesuits* were concerned. Perhaps many Protestants still felt a sneaking lack of confidence in relation to the Roman Catholic Church; certainly, its claims to be the true Church always rankled. Puritans feared Catholic trappings of worship and grew alarmed when Arminian* theologians like John Cosin stressed the value of similar devices as a means to encourage courtiers to stay within the Church of England (**195**).

The 'bogey-man' for Arminians* was Presbyterianism*. Although apparently marginalised by the machinations of Whitgift and Bancroft in the 1580s and '90s, a Presbyterian 'plot' to undermine both Church and state was still a potent myth for Laud and Neile in the 1630s. It obviously still rankled with Peter Heylyn long after the Civil War, for he wrote numerous defences of his Church and a partisan history of Presbyterianism. Where Puritans* feared 'Popery', Arminian intellectuals like John Overall and Lancelot Andrewes felt that Catholicism offered much that was worthy of emulation in its ceremonial notions of worship. Issues like the ordination of ministers, the consecration* of churches, the use of confession, and the nature of ritual in worship were always thorny ones for Protestants. What is interesting in this period is the way in which some theologians began to feel more at ease in their relationship with the Catholic Church. Arminians dared to suggest that the Pope was not Antichrist. They appreciated many aspects of Catholic doctrine and ceremonial, and therefore broke away from the committed anti-popery which had been one of the principal unifying bonds of the Calvinist consensus of the 1590s. It is little wonder that Arminians were seen as 'ushers in of popery' by their enemies; this factor played a crucial part in the origins of the Civil War.

The Church of England in this period was a broad Church, not just one fought over by Arminians* and Puritans* – hence its eventual survival. Many people were caught in the middle ground. Calvinist bishops like Morton and Davenant actually supported some of the ceremonial changes which Puritans found so worrying in the 1630s, such as the erection of altars and bowing at the name of Jesus. Many clergymen from all wings of the Church appreciated the new decorum with which the sacraments were administered. Many revelled in the resurgence of the clerical estate and were adamant that there was nothing wrong in clergymen exercising secular power. Moderates like Hall, Ussher and King found themselves stranded when Parliament finally abolished episcopacy* in 1646. These men were scarcely Arminians, but by that date fears of episcopacy had reached overwhelming proportions and many regarded it as a Papist device for bringing England to ruin. This fear was so acute that opponents of episcopacy felt that once again they were fighting for the Reformation. Hence, the resurrection in the 1640s of old desires to root out scandalous ministers, and to plant all over the land a preaching ministry responsible to the 'godly' (**131, 147, 153, 184**).

Even when we discuss 'Puritans'* and 'Arminians'* we have to be on our guard, since both terms cover a wide range of opinion. That has always been acknowledged as a difficulty with the term 'Puritanism', but also needs to be borne in mind for 'Arminianism'. Anti-Calvinism drew together theologians of many different types and temperaments. Not all were necessarily members of the Arminian 'party' as represented by the 'Durham House'* inner circle led by Neile and Laud. Less 'political' Arminians like Samuel Harsnett and John Howson attained high office under Charles I, but were never really trusted by Neile and his Durham associates. Although once cited for excessive ceremonial at Norwich in 1624, Harsnett was the only bishop to side with erstwhile opponents in voting for the Petition of Right in 1628. If this book has presented a rather unsavoury image of the Arminians, it is because the 'party' rose to power by assiduously courting James I, the Duke of Buckingham, and Charles I. Neile and Laud were shrewd Court politicians. They were ruthless in their appreciation of the need to gain support from civil lawyers*, and to influence university college elections and the composition of cathedral chapters. Our knowledge of Arminianism is coloured by the character and political interests of the 'Durham House' group, and it is necessary to remember less selfish, and more pious figures like Lancelot Andrewes, when thinking of the movement as a whole (**118**).

There is also a problem in dealing with several generations of Arminians*. The first generation of Neile, Andrewes, Laud, and Buckeridge had different interests and experiences from those of the second generation, of Cosin, Lindsell, Mawe, and Wren. The former fought battles even to survive, while the latter were involved in putting their ideas more forcefully into practice. Discussion of Arminianism tends to highlight conflict – hence we think automatically of its part in the origins of the Civil War. It is important, however, to remember other Arminian concerns – close study of the Fathers*, a more ecumenical* stance towards Rome, and an interest in liturgy* – which were influential in the Church restored after 1660. Long-term success should be kept in mind as much as short-term failure.

How do we assess the strength of the Church of England as an institution?

In 1570 the Church of England embraced several Protestant groups all jockeying for control over its doctrines and organisation. The disputes regularly spilled over into Parliament. Although nominally part of this Church, a proportion of the population remained steadfastly Catholic. Between 1584 and 1610 Archbishops Whitgift and Bancroft fashioned a greater sense of organisational unity, whilst Hooker and Andrewes provided the Church of England with a clear and distinctive rationale. Extremists of various persuasions were forced to choose whether or not to remain within this more unified Church, exemplified by the 141 Canons* of 1604. These were a major achievement, and provided a focus for all later discussions within the Church. Through these Canons, the organisation, doctrines, and liturgy* of the Church were secured, even if the hearts and minds of many of its members remained to be won. The intellectual elite had been captured for Protestantism, which in turn had changed from being a religious movement associated with protest in the sixteenth century, into a recognisable and distinctive Church of England in the seventeenth century.

Opinions differ as to the relative contributions of the various archbishops to the success of the Church as an institution. On one reading, Whitgift, Bancroft, and Laud appear to be the strong and successful archbishops. They emphasised the importance of the

Church's organisation and strengthened its bureaucracy; they presided over powerful ecclesiastical courts, held major visitations* and attempted to strengthen the economic base of the Church. On another reading, Grindal and Abbot, with their emphasis on spreading the gospel and leading by example, presided over a Church which gave greater scope to all shades of 'godly' opinion. According to some writers, they offered a vision of a broad 'Anglican' tradition which should have been followed, rather than the narrow and therefore divisive stand adopted by Laud. Most bishops, at least until 1625, shared the ideals of Grindal and Abbot and espoused the model of the 'preaching pastor'. It was after the accession of Charles I and the rise of Arminians* that the image of bishops as 'prelates' changed beyond redemption (**59**).

The success of the Church of England cannot, however, be judged simply by reference to the work of its theologians and the development of Canons*. The assessment becomes more problematical when one turns to look at the meaning of the Church for ordinary people. Many historians have expressed doubts about the universal appeal of Protestantism. Yet all acknowledge that it slowly gained ground, either attributing this to Puritan* evangelicals, or emphasising the irony that this may have occurred precisely because of the greater use of ceremonial permitted in the seventeenth century. That use of ceremonial had the effect of placing all on the same level before God and his ministers, and in consequence may have given rise to social tensions exemplified in the massive rise in seating disputes in parish churches in the seventeenth century.

Whatever the doubts and problems, it does seem as if the Church was gaining a more secure footing with larger numbers of all levels of society than hitherto supposed. Even the much-abused Church courts seem to have played a role in this process by fulfilling the need for social control as well as by acting as instruments of episcopal discipline. Martin Ingram points to the acceptable face of the work of the Church courts and has concluded that

> Over the period 1570–1640 the church courts played a significant part in improving clerical standards. They also helped to marginalise catholic recusants* and to nudge the mass of the population towards more rigorous standards of religious devotion and observance. (**79**, p. 366)

The courts were vulnerable in the 1630s, because of the way in which they were used by the authorities, but they were not directly to blame for their dramatic collapse in the 1640s. Clerical standards were rising and people felt inclined to spend money on their churches. There may have been a slight shift in emphasis from the parish to the household as the key focus of religious life for some, but for the majority the parish community still fulfilled the need for organised worship throughout this period.

The connections between religion and the British Civil War

It is currently fashionable in some quarters to deny the importance of religious factors in the origins of the Civil War. Gardiner's 'Puritan* Revolution' has been abandoned, and the recent stress on the role of Arminianism* questioned by 'revisionists', who prefer to talk only of short-term causes. An emphasis on accidents and personalities has replaced discussion of matters of principle, be they constitutional or religious. Nevertheless, a glance at the Root and Branch petition, the later Grand Remonstrance, and the debates of the Westminster Assembly* reveals many religious grievances which were central to why people eventually went to war. Moreover, the very emphasis recently placed on events after 1638 has given us a greater awareness of religious 'trigger causes' of the war. The existence of three different religions in three kingdoms within the British Isles served to exacerbate a breakdown of government, leading to a 'crisis of multiple kingdoms' (**105**).

The debates about the causes of the war are bound up with different views of long- and short-term causes. Some writers see the war as arising out of a series of accidents occurring during the period 1638–42. Others, possibly still a majority, now hold to the view once expressed by Clarendon, that there is no need to go back beyond the accession of Charles I in 1625 to discover the origins of the war. Such a view accords considerable importance to the work of Laud and his Arminian* associates in changing the relationship between Church and state and Church and people in Charles's reign. Few would now agree with an assessment that sees Elizabeth presiding over a period of calm in Church and state which was destroyed by the foolish Stuarts, but the year 1603 is another candidate for a turning-point of significance. For those who stress the importance of the impact of Arminian ideas, and more particularly, faction, on the Church, we would need to go back to the 1590s to find the origins of problems. So the debate ebbs and flows.

It is the contention of this book that religion played a major part in the origins of the war and operated as a critical factor in many different respects. Religious ideas certainly affected the way in which the educated elite divided in the 1640s. Myths about Arminians*, Catholics and Puritans* fed the emotions of another larger segment of society (**91, 175, 176**). The existence of different religious groups in the kingdoms of England, Scotland, and Ireland has been shown to be a crucial factor at various stages in the short-term origins of the war (**105**). Meanwhile, the existence of what Patrick Collinson has described as 'war on the streets', which was central to Protestant polemic in the battle with the forces of Antichrist, provided background fuel which only needed a spark in the 1640s (**49**). Religious issues precipitated action in the 1640s, they acted as a bond for each of the two sides which eventually formed to fight the Civil War, and they provided legitimation for what followed. It is for these reasons that John Morrill has claimed that 'the English Civil War was not the first European revolution; it was the last of the Wars of Religion' (**176**, p. 178).

Religious ideas and practices were central to one strand which fed the 'competing myths' which led to war; the resurgence of the clerical estate as a force in the land was another. The complaints of the 1640s did not only concentrate on Arminianism*, Popery, and ceremonial innovations. What mattered just as much for many people was the fact that bishops in particular seemed to be regaining secular power lost at the Reformation. Hence the accusations made in the Long Parliament that clergymen were usurping temporal authority, preaching in favour of royal absolutism, slandering the power of Parliament, and using their courts against the interests of the common law. It was for these reasons that Parliament moved so swiftly to curb the rights of clergy to sit on Commissions of the Peace*. Indeed, members of the Long Parliament felt so little sympathy for bishops that they deprived them of their seats in the Lords and subsequently abolished episcopacy* as such [**doc. 27**].

New directions for research?

The Church of England during this period is a rich topic which provides many avenues for research. The question of the part played by religious issues in the origins of the Civil War will always fascinate historians. The focus of attention has been usefully shifted from Puritans* to Arminians*, but much remains to be done before we shall have full illumination on the nature and impact of the policies pursued and implemented in the 1630s. Diocesan studies are under way which will throw light on the effectiveness of Laud and his episcopal colleagues, but investigations at the parish level are also needed before we can test some of the general hypotheses put forward recently. Christopher Haigh has suggested that we have heard too much of '"sermon-gadding" by the godly, and should be more sensitive to "sacrament-gadding" by the rest' (**61,** p. 218). John Morrill's research on the Interregnum suggests that parish congregations showed great loyalty to the Book of Common Prayer and resisted attempts to force them to use the officially authorised Directory of Worship (**97**).

Discussion of 'new' concepts like Arminianism* invariably alters perceptions of 'old' ones such as Puritanism* and Catholicism, and we have become increasingly aware of how useful it is to study the shifting border over which converts travelled in both directions. More work is needed at the parish level to see if there is sufficient evidence of the 'moral panics' detected by David Underdown (**120**), and to test Patrick Collinson's intriguing suggestion that perhaps 'England's wars of religion began, in a sense, with a maypole' (**49,** p. 141). We need to find ways of detecting the views of the 'silent majority' who may indeed have been becoming 'parish Anglicans' during this period, blissfully unconcerned by the theological in-fighting of intellectuals in their midst or of powerful clerical factions at Court.

Part Four: Documents

document 1

Peter Heylyn's opinion of Archbishop Neile

*Peter Heylyn (1599–1662) was a clergyman and controversial writer who
became William Laud's chaplain and later wrote books in defence of his
master. This sketch of Richard Neile, who was in turn Laud's patron,
should be contrasted with that offered by William Prynne. The critical role
of Clerk of the Closet mentioned below entailed some power over the selection
of divines who could preach before the King. Note this perception of the
importance of the Scots at the Court of James I.*

In the beginning of the reign of King James (by the power and
mediation of Bishop Bancroft) he [Neile] was made Clerk of the
Closet to that king, that standing continually at his elbow, he might
be ready to perform good offices to the Church and churchmen:
And he discharged his trust so well, that though he lost the love of
some of the Courtiers, who were too visibly inclined to the Puritan
faction, yet he gained the favour of his Master, by whom he was
preferred to the Deanery of Westminster, and afterwards succes-
sively to the Bishoprics of Rochester, Lichfield and Coventry,
Lincoln and Durham, one of the richest in the kingdom; which
shows that there was in him something more than the ordinary,
which made that king so bountiful and gracious to him. Nor stayed
he there, but by the power and favour of his chaplain, he was
promoted in the reign of King Charles to the see of Winton
[Winchester], and finally exalted to the Metropolitan see of York,
where at last he died about the latter end of October 1640. None
of his chaplains received so much into his counsells as Doctor
Laud (to which degree he was admitted in the year 1608) whom he
found both an active and a trusty servant, as afterwards a most
constant and faithful friend upon all occasions....

Many good offices he had done to the Church and churchmen
in his attendance at the court, crossing the Scots in most of their
suits, their ecclesiastical preferments, which greedily and

82

ambitiously they hunted after, and thereby drawing on himself the general hatred not only of the Scots, but Scotizing English. But of this prelate we have spoke so much upon other occasions, that we may save the labour of any further addition, than that he died as full of years as he was of honours, an affectionate subject to his Prince, an indulgent father to his clergy, a bountiful patron to his chaplains, and a true friend to all which relied upon him; more fortunate in the time of his death than the course of his life, in being prevented by blessed opportunity from seeing those calamities which afterwards fell upon the king, the Church, and all that wish well to either of them; which must have been more grievous to him than a thousand deaths.

P. Heylyn, *Cyprianus Anglicus*, 1668, pp. 59–60, 459–60.

document 2

William Prynne's opinion of Archbishop Neile

William Prynne (1600–69) was a lawyer and inveterate writer on religious affairs. He was pilloried and lost his ears after show trials in 1634 and 1637 on account of his constant attacks on Laud and the Arminians. Note his attitude towards Arminians, Parliament and the causes of the war.

Richard Neale the last Archbishop of York, before his coming to the See, about the 13 yeare of King James not long after hee was created a Bishop, was highly questioned in Parliment for seditious speeches against the Commons House, for which he had suffered condigne punishment, had he not beene an active instrument to dissolve that Parliament, to avoid the censure of it. Since that he had a hand in dissolving other Parliaments, to the prejudice of the King and Kingdome. In the Remonstrance of the Commons House of Parliament, presented to King Charles our Soveraigne in the 3 yeare of his Raigne; hee was by name complained against as one of the chiefe heads of the popish and Arminian Factions, which disquietted both our Church and State; and as a persecutor of good Ministers he prosecuted, silenced, suspended, deprived, both in the High Commission, and all the Diocesse under his Jurisdiction, whiles hee continued in favour at Court, is so well knowne to all, that I need not relate it: ...

He was the first advancer of William Laud Archbishop of Canterbury, of Doctor Cousins, with sundry other Incendiaries and Innovators both in the Church and State, who were entertained by him for his Chaplaines, and then promoted by his meanes, to the ruine almost of our Religion and Kingdome. He was a great enemy to Parliaments, Prohibitions, the Liberties of the Subject, and Lawes of the Land: Hee seldome or never preached himselfe, and therefore could not endure frequent preaching in others: Hee was a great furtherer of the Book for sports on the Lords day, and an enemy to puritie, Puritans, and the sincere practise of pietie.

Hee had a hand in ratifying the late Canons and Oath, an affront of his Majesties Prerogative, the Parliament, Lawes, and Liberties of the Subject; And no doubt he had a finger in the late Scottish Warres and Combustions; whereupon hee burnt all his Letters concerning Church and State-affaires, as soone as he heard the Scots had entred into England, for feare he should have been surprized and his fellow-Prelates machinations against the Scots by their surprisall discovered.

This Prelate being scarce Parliament proofe, to prevent all questioning; at the approach of this present Parliamentary Assembly fell sicke and dyed, being now gone to answer all his Episcopall extravagancies before a greater Tribunall.

W. Prynne, *The Antipathie of the English Lordly Prelacie*, 1641, I, 222–4.

document 3

T. B. Macaulay on Archbishop Laud

The classic 'Whig' damnation of Archbishop Laud.

Of all the prelates of the Anglican Church, Laud had departed farthest from the principles of the Reformation, and had drawn nearest to Rome. His theology was more remote than even that of the Dutch Arminians from the theology of the Calvinists. His passion for ceremonies, his reverence for holidays, vigils, and sacred places, his ill-concealed dislike of the marriage of ecclesiastics, the ardent and not altogether disinterested zeal with which he asserted the claims of the clergy to the reverence of the laity, would have made him an object of aversion to the Puritans, even if he had used only legal and gentle means for the attainment of his ends. But his understanding was narrow, and his commerce with the world had been small. He was by nature rash, irritable, quick to feel for his own dignity, slow to sympathize with the sufferings of others, and prone to the error, common in superstitious men, of mistaking his own peevish and malignant moods for emotions of pious zeal. Under his direction every corner of the realm was subjected to a constant and minute inspection. Every little congregation of separatists was tracked out and broken up. Even the devotions of private families could not escape the vigilance of his spies. Such fear did his rigour inspire that the deadly hatred of the Church, which festered in innumerable bosoms, was generally disguised under an outward show of conformity. On the very eve of troubles, fatal to himself and to his order, the Bishops of several extensive dioceses were able to report to him that not a single dissenter was to be found within their jurisdiction.

T. B. Macaulay, *The History of England*, 3 vols, Everyman edition, 1906, 1, pp. 74–5.

document 4
Christopher Hill on the Church of England

A classic, robust Marxist interpretation of the social and political function of the Church.

The Church throughout the Middle Ages, and down to the seventeenth century, was something very different from what we call a church to-day. It guided all the movements of men from baptism to the burial service, and was the gateway to the life to come in which all men fervently believed. The Church educated children; in the village parishes – where the mass of the people were illiterate – the parson's sermon was the main source of information on current events and problems, of guidance on economic conduct. The parish itself was an important unit of local government, collecting and doling out such pittances as the poor received. The Church controlled men's feelings and told them what to believe, provided them with entertainment and shows. . . .

The Church, then, defended the existing order, and it was important for the Government to maintain its control over this publicity and propaganda agency. For the same reason, those who wanted to overthrow the feudal state had to attack and seize control of the Church. That is why political theories tended to get wrapped up in religious language. . . . As long as the power of the State was weak and uncentralised, the Church with its parson in every parish, the parson with honoured access to every household, could tell people what to believe and how to behave; and behind the threats and censures of the Church were all the terrors of hell fire. Under these circumstances social conflicts inevitably became religious conflicts.

But the fact that men spoke and wrote in religious language should not prevent us realising that there is a social content behind what are apparently purely theological ideas. Each class created and sought to impose the religious outlook best suited to its own needs and interests. But the real clash is between these class interests: behind the parson stood the squire.

It is not then denied that the 'Puritan Revolution' was a religious as well as a political struggle; but it was more than that. What men were fighting about was the whole nature and future development of English society.

Christopher Hill, *The English Revolution 1640*, Lawrence & Wishart, 1940, pp. 11–12.

document 5

Extract from the Millenary Petition of 1603

This well-known document contained requests under four headings: that on the Church service, below; the others on Church ministers, Church livings and maintenance, and Church discipline.

I. *In the Church Service.* That the cross in baptism, interrogatories ministered to infants, confirmation, as superfluous, may be taken away: baptism not to be ministered by women, and so explained: the cap and surplice not urged: that examination may go before the communion: that it be ministered with a sermon: that divers terms of *priests* and *absolution*, and some other used, with the ring in marriage, and other such like in the Book, may be corrected: the longsomeness of service abridged: church songs and music moderated to better edification: that the Lord's Day be not profaned, the rest upon holy-days not so strictly urged: that there may be an uniformity of doctrine prescribed: no Popish opinion to be any more taught or defended: no ministers charged to teach their people to bow at the name of Jesus: that the canonical Scriptures only be read in the church.

J. R. Tanner, *Constitutional Documents of the Reign of James I 1603–1625*, Cambridge University Press, 1952, p. 58.

document 6
Extract from Thomas Wood's letter to the Earl of Leicester, 7 September 1576

Thomas Wood was a great Puritan campaigner not afraid to speak openly to aristocratic supporters, here replying to a letter from Leicester whom Wood had forced to defend his patronage of bishops.

As for the byshops whom your Lordship hath commended, I know not.... Touching the use of them, I will shew your Lordship a godly gentillman's opinion, and now of very good calling, which he was wonte ofte merely [merrily] to utter, thus: 'Let the godliest man, and best learned within this realme be chosen, and put once a rochet on his backe, and it bringeth with it such an infection as that will marr him for ever'. I would experience had not taught this thing to be as true as it was merily spoken. These are they that burden others to be disturbers of the peace of our Church, wherein they have been and are the doers of it. For if they had at the beginning sought a full reformation according to God's word, and an utter abolishing of all Papists' dreges, these controversies had never come into question. But every one sought how to catche a welthy and rich bishopricke, some paying well for it, xxxxl. [£40] pention to some one man during his life, as I have credibly heard. And thus neglecting God's glory, they sought their owne, and therefore God never blest their doings to this day, nor never will so long as they continue in this pompe and great wealth.... Thus with their covetous example, they have done farr more harme than they have done good by their preaching.... But now I will yow of a good byshope indeed. There is not far from Asheby a pore town called Mesham; the most parte there are colliers. They have had one Peter Eglesall, a grave and godly man to their minister not much above a yeare and a halfe, who with his continuall diligence in this time hath brought to passe that there is not one in his parish of lawfull years but they are able by harte to make a good and godly confession of their faith.... And this man hath not of his parish (as I thinke) above xxl. [£20] a yeare, besides a little farme of his owne not far off. I doe feare, my Lord, that all they bishops, deans and chaplens in England are not able in these 19 years by past to shewe forth the like fruites. This is one of those men, my Lord, that is counted precise and curious. The Lord increase the number of them to a thousand thousand, for such they be indeed that have bene both the beginners and cheif maintayners of all the godly exercises. And if the Gosple has had any increase in England these yeares before named, it hath been chiefly by their preaching and godly example of life.

P. Collinson, 'Letters of Thomas Wood, Puritan, 1566–1577', in his collection of essays entitled *Godly People; Essays on English Protestantism and Puritanism*, Hambledon Press, 1983, pp. 101–3.

document 7
Canon thirty-six: Subscription required of such as are to be made Ministers

No person was to be admitted to the ministry, or licensed to preach, teach or lecture until he had signed agreement to the following three articles first promulgated under Archbishop Whitgift and here enshrined as one of the Canons of 1604.

1. That the king's majesty, under God, is the only supreme governor of this realm, and of all other his highness's dominions and countries, as well in all spiritual or ecclesiastical things or causes, as temporal; and that no foreign prince, person, prelate, state, or potentate hath, or ought to have, any jurisdiction, power, superiority, pre-eminence, or authority, ecclesiastical or spiritual, within his majesty's said realms, dominions, and countries.

2. That the Book of Common Prayer, and of ordering of bishops, priests and deacons, containeth in it nothing contrary to the word of God, and that it may lawfully so be used; and that he himself will use the form in the said book prescribed, in public prayer, and administration of the sacraments, and none other.

3. That he alloweth the Book of Articles of Religion agreed upon by the archbishops and bishops of both provinces, and the whole clergy in the convocation holden at London in the year of our Lord God one thousand five hundred sixty and two; and that he acknowledgeth all and every the articles therein contained, being in number nine and thirty, besides the ratification, to be agreeable to the word of God.

E. Cardwell, *Synodalia*, Oxford University Press, 1842, I, pp. 267–8.

document 8
John Selden on the misfortunes of being a clergyman

This is an early, feeble example of a joke in the 'three men' genre, but it serves to illustrate some of the problems faced by ordinary ministers of the Church of England. Remember that prisoners were regarded according to what they might be able to pay their gaolers for perquisites.

The Protestant Minister is least regarded, appears by the old story of the Keeper of the Clink. He had Priests of several sorts sent unto him; as they came in, he asked them who they were; who are you to the first? I am a Priest of the Church of Rome; you are welcome quoth the Keeper, there are those will take care of you, and who are you? A silenced Minister. You are welcome too, I shall fare the better for you: and who are you? A Minister of the Church of England. O God help me (quoth the Keeper) I shall get nothing by you, I am sure you may lie and starve, and rot, before any body will look after you.

J. Selden, *Table-Talk*, 1696 edition, p. 106.

document 9
Extract from articles agreed by the sub-committee for religion in the House of Commons, 24 February 1629

This influential sub-committee, which included John Pym, played an important part in orchestrating parliamentary debates and raising public awareness of Arminianism. Note their connection of events with the much older threat of Popery.

Here in England we observe an extraordinary growth of Popery, insomuch that in some counties, where in Queen Elizabeth's time there were few or none known recusants, now there are above 2,000, and all the rest generally apt to revolt. A bold and open allowance of their religion, by frequent and public resort to mass, in multitudes, without control, and that even to the Queen's Court, to the great scandal of his Majesty's government. Their extraordinary insolence; for instance, the late erecting of a College of Jesuits in Clerkenwell, and the strange proceedings thereupon used in favour of them. The subtle and pernicious spreading of the Arminian faction; whereby they have kindled such a fire of division in the very bowels of the State, as if not speedily extinguished, it is of itself sufficient to ruin our religion; by dividing us from the Reformed Churches abroad, and separating amongst ourselves at home, by casting doubts upon the religion professed and established, which if faulty or questionable in three or four articles, will be rendered suspicious to unstable minds in all the rest, and incline them to popery, to which those tenets, in their own nature, do prepare the way: so that if our religion be suppressed and destroyed abroad, disturbed in Scotland, lost in Ireland, undermined and almost outdared in England, it is manifest that our danger is very great and imminent.

J. P. Kenyon, *The Stuart Constitution*, Cambridge University Press, 1966, p. 157.

document 10
Directions to preachers, 1622

These directions were typical of attempts, which grew more frantic with the later 'Proclamation for Peace and Quiet' of 1626, to control preaching. The orders tried to restrict the number of ministers able to preach, the occasions, times of day, and subject matter of sermons. Ministers were encouraged to use the Book of Homilies *and discouraged, as below, from covering any controversial topics like predestination.*

III. That no preacher of what title so ever under the degree of a Bishop, or Dean at the least, do from henceforth presume to preach in any popular auditory the deep points of predestination, election, reprobation, or of the universality, efficacy, resistibility or irresistibility, of God's grace; but leave those themes rather to be handled by the learned men, and that moderately and modestly by way of use and application rather than by way of positive doctrines, being fitter for the Schools than for simple auditories.

J. R. Tanner, *Constitutional Documents of the Reign of James I 1603–1625*, Cambridge University Press, 1952, p. 81.

document 11
Extract from the Proclamation for the Establishing of the Peace and Quiet of the Church of England, 16 June 1626

The matter of 'innovations' in religion had become very sensitive, and this proclamation is thought by some historians to have been a genuine attempt to stop extremists of all persuasions from squabbling over fine points of theology. Contemporaries wondered what those of 'Durham House' would make of it, but the proclamation probably hurt Calvinists more than Arminians.

His Majesty...hath thought fit, by the advice of his reverend bishops, to declare and publish not only to his own people but also to the whole world his utter dislike to all those who, to show the subtlety of their wit, or to please their own humours, or vent their own passions, do or shall adventure to stir or move any new opinions not only contrary [to] but differing from the sound and orthodoxical grounds of the true religion sincerely professed and happily established in the Church of England; and also to declare his full and constant resolution that neither in matter of doctrine or discipline of the Church, nor in the government of the State, he will admit of the least innovation, but by God's assistance will so guide the sceptre of these his kingdoms and dominions, by the Divine Providence put into his hand, as shall be for the comfort and assurance of his sober, religious and well-affected subjects, and for the repressing and severe punishing of the insolencies of such as out of any sinister respects or disaffection to his person and government shall dare either in Church or state to disturb or disquiet the peace thereof.

J. P. Kenyon, *The Stuart Constitution*, Cambridge University Press, 1966, pp. 154–5.

document 12
Lucy Hutchinson on the inflation of the term 'Puritan'

Wife of Colonel Hutchinson, who held Nottingham for Parliament during the Civil War, Lucy Hutchinson depicts how the term 'Puritan' took on extra meanings and social and political content during this period. She traces events back to the reign of James I.

The payment of civil obedience to the king and the laws of the land satisfied not; if any durst dispute his impositions in the worship of God, he was presently reckoned among the seditious and disturbers of the public peace, and accordingly persecuted; if any were grieved at the dishonour of the kingdom, or the griping of the poor, or the unjust oppressions of the subject, by a thousand ways, invented to maintain the riots of the courtiers, and the swarms of needy Scots the king had brought in to devour like locusts the plenty of this land, he was a puritan; if any, out of mere morality and civil honesty, discountenanced the abominations of those days, he was a puritan, however he conformed to their super-stitious worship; if any showed favour to any godly honest persons, kept them company, relieved them in want, or protected them against violent or unjust oppression, he was a puritan; if any gentleman in his country maintained the good laws of the land, or stood up for any public interest, for good order or government, he was a puritan: in short, all that crossed the views of the needy courtiers, the proud encroaching priests, the thievish projectors, the lewd nobility and gentry – whoever was zealous for God's glory or worship, could not endure blasphemous oaths, ribald conversa-tion, profane scoffs, sabbath breaking, derision of the word of God, and the like – whoever could endure a sermon, modest habit or conversation, or anything good, – all these were puritans; and if puritans, then enemies to the king and his government, seditious, factious hypocrites, ambitious disturbers of the public peace, and finally, the pest of the kingdom.

Lucy Hutchinson, *Memoirs of the Life of Colonel Hutchinson*, Everyman edition, 1968, pp. 64–5.

document 13
Extracts from royal instructions to Archbishop Abbot (1629); re-issued with some additions to Archbishop Laud (1633)

These instructions provide the framework for many of the ecclesiastical policies pursued in the 1630s. Bishops were required to keep residence and provide annual reports on their dioceses; they were to ensure that royal proclamations concerning 'questions in difference be strictly observed', to take special care over the quality of ordinations, and to monitor closely all town lectureships. Note the focus on economic problems of the Church.

IX. That no bishop whatsoever, who by our grace and good opinion of his service shall be nominated by us to another bishopric, shall from the day of our nomination presume to make any lease for three lives or one and twenty years, or a concurrent lease, or any ways renew any estate, or cut any wood or timber, but merely receive the rents due and quit the place: for we think it a hateful thing, that any man's preferment to a better bishopric should almost undo the successor. And if any shall presume to break this order, we will refuse him our royal assent, and keep him at the place which he hath so abused.

X. That every bishop give his metropolitan a strict account yearly of their obedience to our late letters prohibiting them to change any leases from years into lives, and that they fail not to certify, if they find that the dean, or dean and chapter, or any archdeacon or prebendary etc. within their several dioceses have at any time broken our command in any particular contained in the aforesaid letters.

E. Cardwell, *Documentary Annals of the Reformed Church of England,* Oxford University Press, 1844 edition, II, pp. 231–2.

document 14

John Cosin on preaching and the duties of the clergy

An extract from Cosin's sermon preached at the consecration of Francis White as Bishop of Carlisle on 3 December 1626, an occasion made noteworthy not only by what was said, but also by the location of the ceremony at Durham House, London, rather than Lambeth Palace.

I come not here to preach down preaching; but this I wonder at, that preaching now-a-days should be counted our only office, as if we had nothing else to do, and an office independent too, as if we were all Bishops when we preach.... We suffer scandal from them of the Church of Rome in many things; in nothing more than this, that we are sent to preach sermons to the people, as men that had some petty commodities to sell them which, if they liked, they might buy and use; if not, they might leave them alone; that we talk of devotion but live like the careless; that we have a service, but no servants at it; that we have Churches but keep them not like the Houses of God; that we have the Sacraments, but few to frequent them; Confession but few to practise it; finally, that we have all religious duties (for they cannot deny it), but seldom observed; all good laws and Canons of the Church, but few or none kept; the people are made to do nothing; the old discipline is neglected, and men do what they list. It should be otherwise, and our Church intends it otherwise....

P. E. More and F. L. Cross (eds), *Anglicanism,* SPCK, 1962, pp. 361–2.

Some of Thomas Fuller's maxims for a 'Good Bishop'

The reflections of a moderate, harking back to the ideal bishop as a preaching pastor when all had been lost in the 1640s.

3. He is diligent and faithful in preaching the Gospel.

4. Painful, pious, and peaceable ministers are his principal favourites.

10. He meddleth as little as may be with temporal affairs.

11. If called to court, he there doth all good offices.

16. He ever makes honourable mention of foreign Protestant churches.

18. He is hospitable in his house-keeping according to his estate.

T. Fuller, *The Holy State*, 3rd edition, 1652, pp. 265–71.

The Lambeth Articles of 1595

The celebrated attempt by Whitgift to codify Church of England theology on the doctrine of grace. The Queen ordered that the articles be withdrawn, and James and Charles stoutly resisted all later appeals to have these articles, or those promulgated at the Synod of Dort, ratified for England.

1. God from eternity predestined certain men to life and condemned others to death.

2. The moving or efficient cause of predestination to life is not foreseeing of faith, or of perseverance, or of good works, or of any other thing which is in the person predestined, but the will of the good pleasure of God alone.

3. The number of the predestined is prescribed and certain and it cannot be increased or diminished.

4. Those who are not predestined to salvation shall of necessity be damned on account of their sins.

5. A true, living and justifying faith and the sanctifying spirit of God is not extinguished, does not leave or disappear in the elect either finally or totally.

6. The man who has true faith, that is, the aforesaid justifying faith, is certain by the abundance of faith of the remission of his sins and of his eternal salvation through Christ.

7. Saving grace is not attributed, nor communicated and not given to all men by which they may be saved if they so will.

8. No one can come to Christ except [grace] be given to him and except the Father draws him. And all men are not drawn by the Father to come to the Son.

9. It is not appointed that in his own will and power each and every man should be saved.

M. C. Cross, *The Royal Supremacy in the Elizabethan Church*, Allen & Unwin, 1969, p. 205.

document 17
Extracts from the Five Articles of the Dutch Remonstrants

The views of the Dutch Remonstrants [Arminians] expressed in these articles were condemned at the Synod of Dort in 1618. Note the tenor and tone of these statements in relation to the English Lambeth Articles.

1. That God, by an eternal and unchangeable purpose in Jesus Christ his Son, before the foundations of the world were laid, determined to save, out of the human race which had fallen into sin, in Christ, for Christ's sake and through Christ, those who through the grace of the Holy Spirit shall believe on the same his Son and shall through the same grace persevere in this same faith and obedience of faith even to the end; and on the other hand to leave under sin and wrath the contumacious and unbelieving and to condemn them as aliens from Christ. . . .

2. That, accordingly, Jesus Christ, the Saviour of the world, died for all men and for every man, so that he has obtained for all, by his death on the cross, reconciliation and remission of sins; yet so that no one is partaker of this remission except the believers.

5. [On the delicate matter of whether the elect could fall from grace] . . . But for the question whether they are not able through sloth or negligence to forsake the beginning of their life in Christ, to embrace again this present world, to depart from the holy doctrine once delivered to them, to lose their good conscience

and to neglect grace – this must be the subject of more exact enquiry in the Holy Scriptures, before we can teach it with full confidence of our mind.

H. Bettenson, *Documents of the Christian Church*, Oxford University Press, 2nd edition, 1967, pp. 268–9.

document 18

Orders put to Convocation in 1589 for better regulation of the clergy

Early efforts to remedy commonly acknowledged grievances and to draw the sting of Puritan complaints.

1. Single beneficed men were obliged to constant residence, with the exception of prebendaries and royal and noblemen's chaplains...

2. Double beneficed men were to reside an equal proportion of time on each of their cures, and when absent to provide a licensed curate.

3. Beneficed men absent one hundred and twenty days were to keep licensed curates.

4. Scandalous ministers were to be removed, and not readmitted to any cure.

5. No ignorant person unqualified to catechise was to be admitted to any cure.

J. Joyce, *A Constitutional History of the Convocations of the Clergy*, 1855; Gregg Press Reprint, 1967, p. 602.

document 19

Joseph Hall's attempts to mediate between Arminians and Calvinists

It is interesting to see a moderate perspective on the theological disputes of the time, to be reminded that the extremists were probably in a minority, and to see how Montagu's writings were placed in a Dutch context by contemporaries regardless of his protestations that he had never read a word of Arminius in his life.

After not many years setling at home, it grieved my soul, to see our own Church begin to sicken of the same disease which we had endeavoured to cure in our Neighbours; Mr Montagues tart and vehement assertions, of some positions, neer of kin to the Remonstrants of Netherland, gave occasion of raising no small broil in the Church; Sides were taken, Pulpits every where rang of these opinions; but Parliaments took notice of the division, and questioned the Occasioner; Now as one that desired to do all good offices to our dear and common Mother, I set my thoughts on work, how so dangerous a quarell might be happily composed; and finding that mis-taking was more guilty of this dissention, than mis-believing; (since it plainly appeared to me, that Mr Montague meant to express, not Arminius, but B. [i.e. Bishop] Overall, a more moderate and safe Authour, however he sped in delivery of him;) I wrote a little project of Pacification, wherin I desired to rectify the judgement of men, concerning this misapprehended controversy; showing them the true parties in this unseasonable Plea; and because B. Overall went a mid-way, betwixt the two opinions which he held extream, and must needs therefore somewhat differ from the commonly-received tenet in these points, I gathered out of B. Overall on the one side, and out of our English Divines at Dort on the other, such common propositions concerning these five busy Articles, as wherein both of them are fully agreed; All which being put together, seemed unto me to make up so sufficent a body of accorded Truth, that all other questions moved here-abouts, appeared merely superstitious, and every moderate Christian, might find where to rest himself without hazard of Contradiction: These I made bold by the hands of Dr Young the worthy Dean of Winchester, to present to his Excellent Majesty, together with a humble motion of a peaceable silence to be injoyned to both parts, in those other collaterall, and needlesse disquisitions: which if they might befit the Schools of Academicall disputants, could not certainly sound well from the Pulpits of popular Auditories: Those reconciliatory papers fell under the eyes of some Grave Divines on both parts, Mr Montague professed that he had seen them, and would subscribe to them very willingly; others that were contrarily minded, both English, Scotish, and French Divines, profered their hands to a no less ready subscription; so as much peace promised to result, out of that weak and poor enterprise, had not the con-fused noise of the misconstructions of those, who never saw the work, (crying it down for the very Names sake) meeting with the royall verdict of a general Inhibition, buryed it in a secure Silence.

I was scorched a little with this flame, which I desired to Quench; yet this could not stay my hand from thrusting it self, into an hotter fire.

J. Hall, *The Shaking of the Olive Tree*, 1660, 37–9.

document 20
Canon eighteen: a reverence and attention to be used within the church in time of Divine Service

One of the Canons passed by Convocation in 1604, and one which gives comfort to those historians who say that we do not need the concept of Arminianism to explain ceremonial changes, for all that Laud was doing was breathing life into these Canons. That still begs questions about the intentions behind this Canon, why it had not been enforced, and whether to do so in the 1630s would be seen as novel.

In the time of divine service, and of every part thereof, all due reverence is to be used; for it is according to the apostle's rule, *Let all things be done decently and according to order;* answerably to which decency and order, we judge these our directions following: No man shall cover his head in the church or chapel in the time of divine service, except he have some infirmity; in which case let him wear a nightcap or coif. All manner of persons then present shall reverently kneel upon their knees, when the general Confession, Litany, and other prayers are read; and shall stand up at the saying of the Belief, according to the rules in that behalf prescribed in the Book of Common Prayer; and likewise when in time of divine service the Lord Jesus shall be mentioned, due and lowly reverence shall be done by all persons present, as it hath been accustomed; testifying by these outward ceremonies and gestures, their inward humility, Christian resolution, and due acknowledgement that the Lord Jesus Christ, the true eternal Son of God, is the only Saviour of the world, in whom alone all the mercies, graces and promises of God to mankind, for this life, and the life to come, are fully and wholly comprised. None ... shall be otherwise at such times busied in the church, than in quiet attendance to hear, mark, and understand that which is read, preached, or ministered; saying in their due places audibly with the minister, the Confession, the Lord's Prayer, and the Creed; and making such other answers to the public prayers, as are appointed in the Book of Common Prayer: neither shall they disturb the service or sermon, by walking or talking, or in any other way; nor depart out of the church during the time of service or sermon, without some urgent or reasonable cause.

E. Cardwell, *Synodalia*, Oxford University Press, 1842, I, pp. 255–6.

document 21
Extracts from churchwardens' presentments for Felpham parish, diocese of Chichester, 1622

The trials and tribulations of being a churchwarden.

Richard Hall of our parrish, miller, hath bin twice presented already for grinding on the Sabbath day of late, and wee have had noe satisfaction nor does he refrayne the same fault; for on Easter day last, after evening prayer, hee wrought in that kinde. Wee desire therefore that hee may have warning and wee satisfyed.

Wee present Thomas Rogers of our parrishe, alehousekeeper, for keeping company in his house on the Sabbath day, in tyme of divine service, namely John Bolton and Edmund Davy and others, of Bersted, whom the churchwardens found there, and the host at home with them.

Wee present Thomas Greene of our parrishe, blacksmith, for refusing to receave the sacrament at Easter, though wee had 4 communions and sufficient warning given. And this he hath done obstinately, being offended with our minister.

Wee want [i.e. lack] a book of homilyes and a book of cannons.

The walling of our church wanteth repayring, our church doth exceedingly want whiting and beautifying, and our chancell wanteth whiting and paving. They are both very darke and fowle, and wee desire therefore that there may be order given that they may bee repayred with all convenient speed. Mr William Cox, our parson, is to repayre the chancell, and our parrish the church.

Wee present Thomas Greene of our parrish, blacksmith, for uniustly rayling uppon our minister, and that ofttymes, accusing him of dishonesty in his life and doctrine.

Also wee present Francis Moorey of our parrishe, husbandman, for abusing our minister in fowle and filthy termes more than once in his druncken humour.

Wee present John Couper of our parrysh, gentlemen, for fearfully swearing and blaspheming the name of God by many most fearfull oathes. And also for vilely abusing Jeffery Woods, one of the sidesmen, because the said Geffery Woods said hee would present the said John Cooper for some misdemeanours, for which cause and no other John Couper threatned to spend his bloud with Geffery Woods, and reviled him with many vile filthy and oppro-brious termes, calling him rogue and rascall, knave, villayne and divell, and in a beastly manner spitt in his face.

H. Johnstone (ed.), 'Churchwardens' Presentments (17th Century) Part I, Archdeaconry of Chichester', *Sussex Record Society*, XLIX, 1948, pp. 32–3.

document 22
Extracts from Archbishop Neile's report on his Province of York – January 1634– section on the dioceses of Chester and Carlisle

An annual report as required by royal decree, but one which reveals the difficulties of enforcing episcopal authority in the 1630s.

I the last year presented to your Majesty such certificates as I received from my brethren, the Bishops of Chester and Carlisle, in the same form and words as I had from themselves, giving credit to them: but having this last summer visited those dioceses, I find things much differing from the said certificates . . .

2. The public prayers of the Church so generally neglected as if all religion were but a sermon.

3. The Book of Common Prayer so neglected and abused in most places, by chopping, changing, altering, omitting and adding at the Minister's own pleasure, as if they were not bound to the form prescribed. In sundry places, the Book of Common Prayer was so unregarded, that many knew not how to read the Service according to the book. And, as in the public prayers, so likewise in the administration of the Sacraments, the forms, rites and ceremonies prescribed very much neglected; and many were found that thought themselves well deserving and conformable men, though they observed not the book and orders prescribed, so long as they did not oppose them.

6. The disrespect that the ministers have shown of the public prayers of the Church has bred such irreverence in the people that it is a rare thing in many places to see any upon their knees at the reading of the prayers, or (almost), at the receiving of the Sacraments. And some stick not to say that sitting was the fittest gesture both at the prayers and at the Sacrament.

7. It was scarce found in any place that the communion table was placed in such sort that it might appear it was any whit respected; but so placed that boys and others might sit about it and lean upon it. And in many places, by teaching of children in the Church or chancel, the communion table was the place where the boys did all their business, and oftentimes eat their victuals upon it. For redress of which abuses in time to come there is order given. At Chester the Dean and Chapter have placed their communion table where it ought to stand and have decently furnished it. But it is not so at Carlisle.

PRO, SP 16/259/78, ff. 168v–69v.

document 23

Extracts from Brent's report to Archbishop Laud on the Metropolitical Visitation held in 1635

This visitation of the southern province of Canterbury, carried out by Sir Nathaniel Brent, Laud's Vicar-General, provides an interesting snapshot of the state of the Church and the task that lay before Laud and his colleagues. Note the tactics employed by Brent and the tone of his account.

LEWES, July 3 & 4 – Mr Bunyard, Maynard, Russell and Gyles refused in open court to bow at the blessed name of Jesus, being by me questioned for it. After long conference, and late at night, they all submitted, confessing that they were convinced in their opinions, and that hereafter they would observe that law of the church and persuade others to do the like. This caused me to revoke my suspension. I inhibited one Mr Jennings to preach any more for particularising in the pulpit. He called one of his parishioners 'arch-knave' and being questioned by me for it, he answered me that it was but a lively application. The man abused did think he had been called 'notched knave', and fell out with his barber who had lately trimmed him.

GUILDFORD, July 7 – There is much faction in these parts. One Prior, a shoemaker in Guildford, is much suspected to be a conventicler. But he denied it very strongly, and I could prove nothing. Here is much straggling to strange parishes. I have given a strict charge to the churchwardens to present them all for it, and have left order in the office that they shall be severely prosecuted. Much irreverence is used in churches by putting on hats in time of divine service, not kneeling when the Ten Commandments are read, etc., and catechising is much neglected. I have beaten down these abuses as much as possibly I can.

Calendar State Papers Domestic, Charles I, 1635, ed. J. Bruce, 1865, preface, xliii–iv.

document 24
An Exhortation concerning Good Order & Obedience to Rulers and Magistrates

Extract from the Homily on Obedience first printed under Elizabeth in 1562; reprinted by order of James I in 1623.

Almighty God hath created and appointed all things in heaven, earth, and waters, in a most excellent and perfect order. In heaven he hath appointed distinct and several orders and states of archangels and angels. In earth he hath assigned and appointed kings, princes, with other governors under them, in all good and necessary order.... For where there is no right order, there reigneth all abuse, carnal liberty, enormity, sin and babylonical confusion. Take away kings, princes, rulers, magistrates, judges and such estates of God's order, no man shall ride or go by the high way unrobbed, no man shall sleep in his own house or bed unkilled, no man shall keep his wife, children and possessions in quietness, all things shall be common; and there must needs follow all mischief and utter destruction both of souls, bodies, goods and commonwealths. But blessed be God that we in this realm of England feel not the horrible calamities, miseries, and wretched-ness, which all they undoubtedly feel and suffer, that lack this godly order; and praised be God that we know the great excellent benefit of God shewed towards us in this behalf. God hath sent us his high gift, our most dear sovereign lord king James, with a godly, wise, and honourable council, with other superiors and inferiors, in a bountiful order, and godly. Wherefore let us subjects do our bounden duties, giving hearty thanks to God, and praying for the preservation of this godly order. Let us all obey, even from the bottom of our hearts, all their godly proceedings, laws, statutes, proclamations, and injunctions, with all other godly orders.

Certain Sermons or Homilies Appointed to be Read in Churches, Oxford University Press, 1840 edition, pp. 95–6.

document 25

Extract from the Declaration on Sports, 1618 and 1633

This declaration gave offence to Puritans anxious to preserve the sanctity of the Lord's Day, but could be seen as a way of courting popularity and denying Catholic accusations that Protestantism was a religion for 'killjoys'.

And as for our good people's lawful recreation, our pleasure likewise is, that after the end of Divine Service our good people be not disturbed, letted, or discouraged from any lawful recreation; such as dancing, either men or women, archery for men, leaping, vaulting, or any other such harmless recreation, nor from having of May-games, Whitsun-ales, and morris-dances, and the setting up of May-poles and other sports therewith used, so as the same be had in due and convenient time, without impediment or neglect of Divine Service; and that women shall have leave to carry rushes to the church for the decoring [i.e. decorating] of it, according to their old custom. But withal we do here accompt still as prohibited all unlawful games to be used up on Sundays only, as bear and bull-baitings, interludes, and at all times in the meaner sort of people by law prohibited, bowling.

J. R. Tanner, *Constitutional Documents of the Reign of James I 1603–1625,* Cambridge University Press, 1952, pp. 55–6.

document 26

Canon five of the seventeen new Canons of 1640

These celebrated Canons were passed by Convocation after the dissolution of the Short Parliament. They included a strong defence of the Divine Right of Kings, commendations for some recent 'innovations' such as the placing of communion tables as altars, a series of Canons about accepted abuses in the ecclesiastical courts, and the following Canon which seems to place all nonconformists in the ranks of 'sectaries'.

Whereas there is provision now made by a canon for the suppressing of popery and the growth thereof, by subjecting all popish recusants to the greatest severity of ecclesiastical censures in that behalf; this present synod well knowing, that there are other sects which endeavour the subversion both of the doctrine and discipline of the Church of England, no less than papists do, although by another way; for the preventing thereof, doth hereby decree and ordain, that all those proceedings and penalties which are mentioned in the aforesaid canon against popish recusants, as far as they shall be appliable, shall stand in full force and vigour against all Anabaptists, Brownists, Separatists, Familists, or other sect or sects, person or persons whatsoever, who do or shall either obstinately refuse, or ordinarily, not having a lawful impediment (that is for the space of a month) neglect to repair to their parish churches or chapels where they inhabit, for the hearing of divine service established, and of receiving the holy Communion . . .

And further, because there are sprung up among us a sort of factious people, despisers and depravers of the book of Common Prayer, who do not according to the law resort to their parish church or chapel to join in the public prayers, service, and worship of God with their congregation, contenting themselves with the hearing of sermons only, thinking thereby to avoid the penalties due to such as wholly absent themselves from the church. We therefore, for the restraint of all such wilful contemners or neglecters of the service of God, do ordain that the church or chapelwardens, and questmen, or sidesmen of every parish, shall be careful to enquire out all such disaffected persons, and shall present the names of all such delinquents at all visitations . . .

E. Cardwell, *Synodalia*, Oxford University Press, 1842, I, pp. 400–2.

document 27
Sections from the Root and Branch Petition, 1640

This was presented to Parliament on 11 December 1640 and effectively summarised grievances against the Crown, notably these on religion.

A Particular of the manifold evils, pressures, and grievances caused, practised and occasioned by the Prelates and their dependents.

2. The faint-heartedness of ministers to preach the truth of God, lest they should displease the prelates; as namely, the doctrine of

predestination, of free grace, of perseverance, of original sin remaining after baptism, of the sabbath, the doctrine against universal grace, election for faith foreseen, free-will against antichrist, non-residents, human inventions in God's worship; all which are generally withheld from the people's knowledge, because not relishing to the bishops.

3. The encouragement of ministers to despise the temporal magistracy, the nobles and gentry of the land; to abuse the subjects, and live contentiously with their neighbours, knowing that they, being the bishops' creatures, shall be supported.

6. The great increase of idle, lewd and dissolute, ignorant and erroneous men in the ministry, which swarm like the locusts of Egypt over the whole kingdom; and will they but wear a canonical coat, a surplice, a hood, bow at the name of Jesus, and be zealous of superstitious ceremonies, they may live as they list, confront whom they please and vent what errors they will, and neglect preaching at their pleasures without control.

7. The discouragement of many from bringing up their children in learning; the many schisms, errors, and strange opinions which are in the Church; great corruptions which are in the Universities; the gross and lamentable ignorance almost everywhere among the people; the want of preaching ministers in very many places both of England and Wales; the loathing of the ministry, and the general defection to all manner of profaneness.

9. The hindering of godly books to be printed . . .

10. The publishing and venting of Popish, Arminian, and other dangerous books and tenets; as namely, 'That the Church of Rome is a true Church, and in the worst times never erred in fundamentals;' 'that the subjects have no propriety in their estates, but that the King may take from them what he pleaseth;' 'that all is the King's, and that he is bound by no law;' . . .

25. Yea further, the pride and ambition of the prelates being boundless, unwilling to be subject either to men or laws, they claim their office and jurisdiction to be *Jure Divino*, exercise ecclesiastical authority in their own names and rights, and under their own seals, and take upon them temporal dignities, places and

offices in the Commonwealth, that they may sway both swords.

J. Rushworth, *Historical Collections*, 1721 edition, IV, pp. 93–5.

document 28

Cartoon lampooning the Court of High Commission

Note how this selects Laud and Matthew Wren, plus the civil lawyers Duck and Lambe, and the celebrated et cetera *oath, for special attention.*

Thomas Stirry, *A Rot amongst the Bishops or a Terrible Tempest in the Sea of Canterbury*, 1641.

document 29

Extracts from William Barlow's *Sum and Substance of the Conference* held at Hampton Court in 1604

This eloquent piece of propaganda was designed to present Puritans in a bad light and to negate the idea that this conference had been necessary or useful in the making of ecclesiastical policy. Yet it serves to reveal the King's strong involvement in the Conference and his concern for unity.

... So admirably, both for understanding, speech, and judgement, did his Majesty handle all those points, sending us away not with contentment only but astonishment, and, which is pitiful you will say, with shame to us all that a King brought up among Puritans, not the learnedest men in the world, and schooled by them; swaying a kingdom full of business and troubles; naturally given to much exercise and repast; should in points of Divinity shew himself as expedite and perfect as the greatest scholars and most industrious students there present might not outstrip him. But this one thing I might not omit, that his Majesty should profess, howsoever he lived among Puritans and was kept for the most part as a ward under them, yet since he was of the age of his son, ten years old, he ever disliked their opinions.

... the end of the conference meet to be had, he [James] said, by every King at his first entrance to the crown; not to innovate the government presently established, which by long experience he had found accomplished with so singular blessings of God 45 years as that no Church upon the face of the earth more flourished than this of England. But first, to settle an uniform order through the whole Church. Secondly, to plant unity, for the suppressing of Papists and enemies to religion. Thirdly, to amend abuses, as natural to bodies politic and corrupt man as the shadow to the body...

... To the second general point, concerning the planting of ministers learned in every parish, it pleased his Majesty to answer, that he had consulted with his Bishops about that, whom he found willing and ready to second him in it, inveighing herein against the negligence and carelessness which he heard of many in this land; ... Therefore this matter was not for a present resolution, because to appoint to every parish a sufficient minister were impossible; the Universities would not afford them. Again, he had found already that he had more learned men in this realm than he had sufficient maintenance for; so that maintenance must first be provided, and then the other to be required.

J. R. Tanner, *Constitutional Documents of the Reign of James I 1603–1625*, Cambridge University Press, 1952, pp. 61–2, 64.

document 30

Thomas Fuller's account of the York House Conference, 1626

A moderate's perspective on a conference which now arouses some debate amongst historians, but which has been acknowledged as possibly as signifi-cant in its way as the Hampton Court Conference of 1604. The debate about Arminianism was now firmly in the public arena, Richard Montagu's tracts had clearly polarised clergymen and laity alike, and this conference made Neile and Laud feel secure in the support of the Duke of Buckingham.

A few days after, (February 6th) a parliament began, wherein Mr Mountagu was much troubled about his book, but made a shift, by his powerful friends, to save himself. During the sitting where-of, at the instance and procurement of Robert Rich, earl of Warwick, a Conference was kept in York-house, February 11th, before the duke of Buckingham and other lords, betwixt Dr Buckeridge, bishop of Rochester, and Dr White, dean of Carlisle, on the one side; and Dr Morton, bishop of Coventry, and Dr Preston, on the other, about Arminian points, and chiefly the possibility of one elected to fall from grace. The passages of which Conference are variously reported. For it is not in tongue-combats, as in other battles, where the victory cannot be disguised, as discovering itself in keeping the field, number of the slain, captives and colours taken. Whilst here, no such visible effects appearing, the persons present were left to their liberty to judge of the conquest as each one stood affected. However, William earl of Pembroke was heard to say, that none returned Arminians thence, save such who repaired thither with the same opinions.

Soon after, (February 17th) a second Conference was enter-tained, in the same place, on the same points, before the same persons.... The passages also of this Conference are as differently related as the former; some making it a clear conquest on one, some on the other, side, and a third sort, a drawn battle betwixt both. Thus the success of these meetings answered neither the commendable intentions nor hopeful expectations of such who procured them.... these Conferences betwixt divines rather increase the differences than abate them.

Thomas Fuller, *The Church History of Britain*, 1842 edition, III, 435–6.

Chronology

Dates	Catholicism	Puritanism	C of E/New theology
1570	Papal bull excomm. and deposed Queen	Cartwright lost Camb. chair; Whitgift's statutes accepted	
1571	Parl. leg. v. recusants: treason to deny royal supremacy; Ridolfi plot	Strickland's bill in Parl. to amend prayer book	Moves to tighten subscription; Canons ratified by Parl.
1572	Duke of Norfolk executed	*Admonitions* presented to Parl.; Field & Wilcox imprisoned; Cartwright lost his fellowship	
1573		Proclam. to end *Admon.* controversy	Whitgift replied to *Admonition*
1574	First priests arrived in England from Douai	Walter Travers wrote in favour of Presbyterianism	
1575			**Abp Matthew Parker died**
1576			**Edmund Grindal apptd Abp of Cant.**; new Canons on quality of clergy
1577		Royal orders suppressed prophesyings	Grindal suspended; Aylmer Bp of London; Whitgift Bp Worcester
1579	English Jesuit college founded in Rome		
1580	Edmund Campion and Robert Parsons led Jesuit mission to England.	Proclam. v. 'Family of Love' sect	
1581	New penal laws: £20 fine for not attending church, conversion = treason; Campion executed		

Dates	Catholicism	Puritanism	C of E/New theology
1582		Dedham 'Classic' met; Brownists now 'separating'	
1583	Throckmorton plot led to expulsion of Spanish ambassador Mendoza	Subscription to 3 Articles required by Whitgift	**Grindal died; Whitgift new Abp;** High Commission revived
1584	William Allen pub. *Defence of English Catholics*	Burghley criticised Whitgift for 'Roman Inquisition' tactics and *ex officio* oath; Puritan surveys debated in Parl.; Emmanuel Coll., Camb. est.	Whitgift allowed use of 3 Articles; Harsnett gave controversial sermon on Predestination
1585	New Recusancy laws; war with Spain; Jesuits expelled	'Association' formed to protect Queen.	
1586	Babington conspiracy	Field and Travers work on *Book of Discipline* – rows in Parl.	Star Chamber decree on censorship; Whitgift apptd to Privy Council
1587	Mary Q of Scots executed; stiff land fines on recusants; William Allen a Cardinal	Cope's 'Bill and Book' in Parl.; Greenwood and Barrow before High Comm.	Bridge's *Defence of Gov. of C. of E.* pub.
1588	Armada defeated	Field and Leicester died; *Martin Marprelate tracts* pub.	Welsh Bible pub.
1589		Puritan petitions to Parl. and Convocation	Lancelot Andrewes Master of Pembroke Coll., Camb.; Bancroft's sermon at Paul's Cross implied *jure divino* episcopacy
1590		Udall tried for *Demonstration of Discipline*; Cartwright in prison; Walsingham died	Adrian Saravria wrote in favour of English clerical orders
1591		Perkins' *The Golden Chain* pub.	

Dates	Catholicism	Puritanism	C of E/New theology
1593		Barrow and Greenwood executed; likewise Penry for *Martin Marprelate tracts*	Bancroft, Bilson and Cosen wrote v. Puritans
1594	Cardinal Allen died		
1595	'Wisbech stirs' amongst Catholic priests	Bound's *Treatise of the Sabbath* pub.	William Barrett's sermon in Camb. led Whitgift to issue Lambeth Articles
1596		Sidney Sussex Coll., Camb. founded	Baro drawn into Camb. controversy and lost Chair
1597			Bancroft Bsp of London
1598	Appt of Archpriest Wm Blackwell sparked controversy		John Overall, Master St Catherine's Coll., Camb.; Howson preached v. Puritans at Paul's Cross
1599			Overall in predestination dispute at Camb.
1600	Secular priests appealed to Rome		Scottish bishops chosen; stormy Commencement ceremonies at Camb.
1602	Proclamation offered concessions to Catholics if took Oath of Allegiance		Whitgift organised survey of churches; Overall Dean of St Paul's
1603	**Elizabeth I died; succeeded by James;** Main and Bye plots	Cartwright died; Millenary Petition	
1604	Peace with Spain	Hampton Court Conf. recorded in Barlow's *Sum and Substance*	**Whitgift died; Bancroft new Abp**; Act to prevent exchange of church lands; 141 new Canons passed by Convocation; Subscription campaign ensued

Dates	Catholicism	Puritanism	C of E/New theology
1605	Gunpowder Plot		
1606	New penal laws on Communion and Oath of Allegiance		
1607			Disputes between civil and common lawyers over 'Prohibitions' and Cowell's *Interpreter*
1608	*Apology* v. Bellarmine pub. in King's name		
1609	*Premonition* v. Bellarmine pub. in King's name		James drawn into Prohibitions controversy
1610			Scottish bishops consec.; **Bancroft died;** Cowell's *Interpreter* burned
1611		King James authorised version of Bible pub.	**Abbot new Abp**; Laud President St John's Coll., Oxf.
1612		Legat and Wightman last heretics burned in Eng.	
1614		'Addled Parl.' witnessed anticlericalism	
1615	'Spanish Match' policy proceeding	Calvinist Irish Canons ratified	Robert Abbot Bp of Salisbury; Howson and Laud attacked at Court
1616		'Commendams' case saw fall of Coke	Lancelot Andrewes on Privy Council; Laud Dean of Gloucester
1617			Richard Neile Bp Durham; Gloucester 'altar affair'

Dates	Catholicism	Puritanism	C of E/New theology
1618	'Book of Sports' issued; Raleigh executed to appease Spain; outbreak of 30 Years' War raised tensions	Carlton, Davenant and Ward sent to Synod of Dort; Selden wrote *History of Tithes*	5 Articles of Perth intro. ceremonies in Scotland; Overall Bp Norwich; Andrewes nom. to Winchester
1619		Calvinists won at Synod of Dort; English under pressure to ratify results	Orders to universities over 3 Articles and preaching; Overall d. but replaced by Harsnett as Bp Norwich
1620	Secret 'Spanish Match' Treaty clinched by Gondomar	'Pilgrim Fathers' sailed for New England in *Mayflower*	Concern expressed on condition of St Paul's Cathedral
1621	Fund raising for Palatinate fuelled anti-Catholicism	Corruption cases involving church courts and officials heard in Parl.	Wm Laud Bp St David's; J. Williams Bp Lincoln and Lord Keeper; Abbot committed manslaughter
1622	Spalato case and Fisher/Laud debate highlighted dangers of conversion		Donne preached in favour of Directions to preachers over Predestination
1623	Fears of 'Spanish Match' heightened as penal laws relaxed and Charles in Spain	Proclamation on control of print and dispersal of books	
1624	War with Spain; marriage treaty with France still raised Catholic hopes		Storm in Parl. over Harsnett's work at Norwich and Montagu's *New Gagg*
1625	**Death of James I; Charles I succeeded** and married Henrietta Maria	Feoffees for Impropriation est. in London	Scottish Act of Revocation affected ecclesiastical lands; row over Montagu's *Appello Caesarem* but he became a royal chaplain

Dates	Catholicism	Puritanism	C of E/New theology
1626	Proclamation allowed recusants to 'compound' for estate fines	Proclamation for 'Peace and Quiet in Church of England'; Puritans outmanoeuvred as Arminians helped to elect Buckingham as Chancellor of Camb.	York House Conference pitted Morton and Preston v. White and Buckeridge on Arminianism; Laud Bp Bath and Wells; White Bp Carlisle
1627	Cosin's *Hours of Prayer* pub. for court ladies		Laud & Neile apptd to Privy Council; Sibthorpe and Manwaring preached for Forced Loan; Abbot sequestered
1628		Uproar in Commons as Neile and Laud called Arminians traitors; Leighton pub. *Appeal to Parliament*; Smart sermon drew attention to innovations at Durham	Neile Bp Winchester; Laud Bp London; Montagu Bp Chichester; Buckeridge Bp Ely
1629	Peace with France	Speaker held in chair as first of 3 resolutions condemned Arminianism	Proclamation for better maintenance of churches; royal orders on lectures
1630	Peace with Spain	Leighton in trouble for *Sion's Plea*	Laud Chancellor of Oxford
1631			Commission for repair of St Paul's Cathedral
1632			Richard Neile, Abp York and commenced Metro. visitation with Easdall
1633	'Book of Sports' reissued	Feoffees for Impropriation disbanded	**Abbot died and Laud Abp Cant.;** Juxon Bp London; 'St Gregory's altar affair'

Dates	Catholicism	Puritanism	C of E/New theology
1634		Prynne pilloried for *Histriomastix*	Metro. visitation of south began under Brent; new orders on leasing policy; new Irish Canons
1635			Matthew Wren Bp Hereford then Norwich; White and Heylin pub. books on the Sabbath
1636	George Con arrived on papal mission to Eng.; Panzani met Montagu	Prynne pub. *A Looking Glass* and *?News from Ipswich*	Juxon apptd Lord Treasurer and to Privy Council; new Scottish liturgy ratified
1637		Prynne, Burton and Bastwick pilloried; riots in Edinburgh; Prynne's *Quench Coale* attacked altar policy	Validity of visitations disputed; Bp Williams suspended; Proclamation to control emigration
1638	Mary de Medici, Queen's mother, arrived in England	Scots drew up national covenant; Glasgow assembly abolished bishops	Wren gained Ely and Montagu Bp of Norwich
1639		Scots invasion led to pacification of Berwick	
1640		Long Parl. in November; Root and Branch petition; Scots invaded again	17 new Canons passed in Convocation April/May; Laud arrested
1641		High Commission abolished; bishops deprived of votes in Lords	Laud impeached; 12 bishops arrested; Root and Branch bill passed
1642	Civil War broke out		

Glossary

Adiaphora   'Matters indifferent' – not considered central to faith.

Admonition controversy   Tracts presented to Parliament in 1572 calling for a Presbyterian structure for the Church, written by Thomas Wilcox, Thomas Field, and Thomas Cartwright. John Whitgift replied before Elizabeth I curtailed debate.

Advowson   Right to nominate a clergyman for a living.

Appellant controversy   Refers to a group of secular priests who appealed to Rome against the appointment of a Jesuit as Archpriest in England and who were also prepared to negotiate with Cecil over a limited oath of allegiance. The dispute lasted from 1598 to 1603.

Archdeaconry   Administrative sub-division of a diocese supervised by an archdeacon.

Arches, court of   Appeals court for the southern province of Canterbury.

Arminian   Principally a term attached to one who questioned Calvinist doctrine on predestination and therefore seemed to give more allowance for free will. Came to be more loosely attached in England to those who ·expressed an interest in the sacraments and ceremonial, while downplaying the role of preaching in worship. Became a term of abuse to mean 'ushers-in of popery', strongly associated with a tight-knit faction in the Church led by Neile and Laud; the Durham House group.

Articles of Perth, 1618   Five articles which introduced greater ceremonial into the Church of Scotland. Swiftly abolished by the Covenanters in 1638.

Assurance   Certainty that the believer is saved.

Benefice   An ecclesiastical living.

Book or Declaration of Sports   Royal orders endorsing certain 'recreations' which could be held on the Sabbath. First issued for Lancashire in 1617, then generally in 1618, and re-issued in 1633, when clergymen had to endorse it from the pulpit.

Brownist   Follower of Thomas Browne (*c.* 1553 –1633), the one-time separatist.

Canons   Ecclesiastical laws established by order of Convocation. Famous examples include those made in 1604 and 1640, but also the Irish Canons of 1615 and 1634.

Catechism   Simplified method of instruction or manual, with basic questions about Christian beliefs, used as a basis for Confirmation classes.

Churchwardens   Lay officers of the parish church, usually elected in twos or threes annually. Responsible for keeping accounts, church maintenance, and presenting parishioners, if guilty of offences, most notably at times of visitation.

Civil lawyers   Lawyers trained in Roman law who administered the Church courts.

Clerk of the Closet   Royal chaplain responsible for drawing up rota of Court preachers.

Commencement ceremonies   Divinity disputations held at Cambridge to decide the award of doctoral degrees.

Commissions of the Peace   Royal commissions conferring authority on Justices of the Peace who presided over Quarter Sessions.

Consecration   Ceremony marking the first appointment of a bishop, or first use of religious articles, church, or land.

Consistory court   Principal diocesan court.

Conventicles   Unauthorised Puritan assemblies.

Convocation   General assembly of the clergy, consisting of an upper and lower house, which met at the same time as Parliament.

Curate   Assistant to a beneficed clergyman.

Delegates, court of   Major appeals court for both ecclesiastical provinces.

Dilapidations   Term for lack of maintenance of ecclesiastical property – could lead to a 'dilapidations suit' when a new incumbent sued his predecessor for damages.

Durham House group   Group associated with Richard Neile after he became Bishop of Durham in 1617. Laud, Buckeridge, and Neile's chaplains, Cosin and Lindsell, were amongst those who frequently congregated at his London residence, Durham House in the Strand.

Elect   The 'few' destined to be saved in Calvinist view of salvation.

Episcopacy   System of Church government by bishops; i.e., the episcopate.

Erastianism   Theory that the Church was subordinate to the state.

Essex Annulment case   The annulment in 1613 of the marriage of the Earl of Essex and Frances Howard, Countess of Essex, when the latter wanted to marry Robert Carr, the King's Scottish favourite who became Earl of Somerset.

Excommunication   Technically the most severe sentence that could be passed by an ecclesiastical court because it banned offenders from participation in Church life.

Exercises   Meetings to discuss the Bible and matters of doctrine.

Ex officio oath   Oath administered to all defendants accused of serious offences in Church courts. Required them to swear to answer truthfully before they knew the charges against them.

Fathers   Early saints and leading theologians (for example, St Augustine, Origen and Cyprian) whose writings were 'rediscovered' by Arminian intellectuals and used as a link with what they believed to be the purer Catholic Church of the ancient world.

Feoffee   A trustee.

Feoffees for Impropriations   A group of Calvinist lay and clerical trustees who purchased impropriations and advowsons in order to present livings to suitable incumbents. Active in the 1620s, suppressed 1633.

First fruits   Payment in tax to the Crown of revenue equal to first year's income.

Glebe   Land attached to the parish which supplied income for the minister. Either farmed directly or rented out. Glebe terriers were surveys of such land.

Hampton Court Conference   Ecclesiastical conference called by James I in 1604, partly in response to the Millenary Petition.

High Commission   Commission for causes ecclesiastical with wide-ranging powers, originally to search out and prosecute Catholic recusants and later all non-conformists. Made up of senior clergymen, civil lawyers, and laymen appointed by the Crown. The best-known was based in London, but there were other regional commissions.

Homily   Prescribed discourse to be read regularly by the parish minister to his congregation.

Impropriation/appropriation   Income from a benefice acquired after the dissolution of the monasteries by both laymen and clerics. Impropriations were also held by the Crown, the Church, the universities, and corporations.

In commendam   Where more than one benefice was held at the same time by special licence, usually as a way of supplementing income.

Incumbent   Holder of an ecclesiastical benefice.

Irenical/ecumenical   Attempting to unite different groups and viewpoints. It implies moderation and mediation of difficult theological points and a willingness to compromise.

Jesuits   Members of the Society of Jesus, a Catholic religious order founded by St Ignatius Loyola in 1540.

Lambeth Articles   Nine articles on predestination issued by Whitgift in 1595, immediately suppressed by Queen Elizabeth.

Lectureships   Posts established, often by town corporations, to promote preaching; cut across normal parish structures.

Liturgy   Form of public worship, hence Church services.

Metropolitical visitation   Visitation of a whole province carried out for an archbishop.

Minor Orders   Lowest offices of the pre-Reformation ministry; for example, porters and acolytes, which were stages towards full ordination.

Oath of Allegiance   Oath of loyalty to the Crown; in particular, the oath prescribed by statute in 1606. This was designed to woo 'moderate' Catholics, to drive a wedge between them and hardliners responsible for the Gunpowder Plot.

Ordinand   Candidate for ordination.

Perambulation   Tradition of 'beating the parish bounds', held at Rogationtide and often associated with community festivities.

Perseverance   Belief that it was impossible for the elect to fall from grace.

Pluralism   Practice of holding more than one Church position at the same time, hence often leading to non-residence.

Prebendary   Holder of a prebend or living of a cathedral.

Predestination   Doctrine highlighted by Calvin and his followers concerning who would be saved and who would be damned. There were different forms of this belief, the most extreme being 'double predestination'. Here God not only predestined those who were to be saved, but also those who were to fall, making him, arguably, author of both good and evil.

Presbyterian   One who believed in a system of Church government organised by lay elders, deacons, pastors, and teachers rather than by bishops.

Presentments   Charges made by churchwardens against people whom they 'presented' (i.e., accused) in response to visitation articles.

Probate   The process of officially proving the validity of a will.

Proclamation for Peace and Quiet, 1626   Proclamation issued in an attempt to curb theological debate on controversial matters such as predestination.

Prophesyings   Meetings of local clergy to discuss scripture, part of the discussion taking place before a lay audience.

Puritanism   'It was not the name of a religion or denomination, still less of a political party or social class. For many decades, it was principally a term of more or less vulgar abuse' (**48**, p.7); otherwise, the 'godly', 'professors of true religion', the 'hotter sort of Protestants' or 'protestants scared out of their wits'. Grounded in the circumstances of the making of the Elizabethan Church, Puritanism became a 'social ethic' by the seventeenth century, characterised by great regard for preaching, education, and a godly life entailing respect for morals, good behaviour, and the Sabbath. Puritans were often consumed by an urge for 'reformation of manners' and saw themselves beset by trials in an evil world.

Rector   Clergyman or layman who received the great tithes due from a benefice.

Recusants   Those who wilfully refused to attend Protestant services; a term commonly used of Catholics.

Reprobation   God's condemnation of those he had not chosen or 'elected' for salvation.

Rites of passage   Religious rituals marking important stages in life, such as baptism.

Rogationtide   Solemn supplication of saints chanted on the three days before Ascension Day.

Roman law   Civil rather than common law.

Sabbatarianism   Practice of keeping Sunday holy and refraining from all work and leisure, devoting the day to worship in various forms.

Sacerdotal   Concept of the sacrificial functions of the priesthood. ·

Secular priests   Catholic clergy not bound by any special order or monastic rule.

Glossary

Sequestration   Where an income or office is temporarily diverted into other hands.

Spiritualities   Income derived from spiritual office.

Subscription campaigns   Periodic campaigns for greater conformity – as in 1583 and 1604 – launched by archbishops and bishops, usually requiring all clergy to subscribe to the Three Articles.

Surplice   Long, loose, white vestment worn by the clergy over a cassock.

Synod of Dort 1618 –19   Synod held at Dordrecht in the Netherlands to discuss the beliefs of Dutch Remonstrants or Arminians about predestination. Dutch Calvinists gained a strong re-affirmation of orthodox opinion in articles issued at the end of the conference, thanks largely to the political support of the powerful Orange family. Foreign delegations were invited, hence the presence of the English led by George Carleton, Bishop of Llandaff.

Synods   Meetings of the clergy.

Temporalities   Lands and property held by the clergy of the King, by dint of secular service.

Three Articles   See **Doc. 7**.

Tithes   Payments made by the laity to the parish church of one-tenth of their income. 'Great tithes', those which went to the rector, normally stemmed from corn, hay, and wood. 'Small tithes' were paid to vicars.

Translation   Preferment from one bishopric to another, usually promotion.

Vestiarian controversy   A dispute about clerical dress, particularly the surplice. *The Advertisements*, drawn up by Archbishop Parker in 1566 on the order of Queen Elizabeth, laid down minimum requirements. Objected to by many Puritans.

Vestments   Robes worn by the clergy when conducting services.

Via media   Middle way.

Vicar   Priest or minister serving in a parish where the revenues had been appropriated, and in consequence receiving only a stipend as income.

Visitation   Inspection of a diocese or archdeaconry by a bishop, chancellor, or archdeacon.

Westminster Assembly   Meetings of a group of Calvinist divines held between 1643 and 1649 under the auspices of Parliament. It produced *The Directory for Public Worship*, which was intended to replace the old *Book of Common Prayer*.

Wisbech stirs   Controversies occasioned when Jesuit discipline was introduced for all Catholic prisoners held at Wisbech Castle in the 1590s, highlighting differences between Jesuits and secular priests.

Writs of prohibition   Writs served by one court against another, prohibiting a case to be heard on the grounds that the court had no authority to try it. Used to transfer cases from a Church court to a common law court – for example, the King's Bench.

York House Conference   Conference held in 1626 at York House, the Duke of Buckingham's London residence, at the request of various Calvinist aristocrats wishing to challenge aspects of Arminian theology.

'Cast of Characters'

Abbot, George (1562–1633)   Calvinist; Abp of Canterbury from 1611.

Abbot, Robert (1560–1617)   Calvinist Regius Prof. of Divinity, Oxford, 1612. Brother of above; became Bp of Salisbury in 1615.

Alabaster, William (1567–1640)   Theologian and poet who converted to Rome, but returned to the Church of England.

Andrewes, Lancelot (1555–1626)   Inspirational Arminian preacher and scholar. Bp of Winchester in 1619.

Arminius, Jacobus (*c.* 1559–1609)   Dutch theologian who challenged Calvinist orthodoxy on the nature of predestination.

Aylmer, John (1521–94)   Supporter of Whitgift; became Bp of London in 1577.

Bancroft, John (1574–1640)   Arminian nephew of Richard Bancroft; Bp of Oxford in 1632.

Bancroft, Richard (1544–1610)   Strong anti-Puritan; disciplinarian, who became Abp of Canterbury in 1604. Formed strong alliance with Robert Cecil at Jacobean Court.

Barlow, William (d. 1613)   Moderate Calvinist writer against Catholics; Bp of Lincoln in 1608.

Baro, Peter (1534–99)   French academic; Lady Margaret Professor of Divinity at Cambridge 1574; retired after disputes in 1595.

Barrett, William   Arminian; fled to Continent and embraced Catholicism after disputes of 1595 over predestination.

Bastwick, John (1593–1654)   Calvinist physician and writer who was pilloried along with Burton and Prynne in 1636 for opposition to Laud.

Bayley, Lewis (d. 1631)   Moderate Calvinist, author of popular *Practice of Piety*; became Bp of Bangor in 1616.

Beza, Theodore (1519–1605)   Succeeded Calvin in Geneva as leader of Calvinists in 1564.

Brent, Sir Nathaniel (*c.* 1573–1652)   Lawyer; Vicar-General to Abp of Canterbury; later sided with Parliament.

Bridges, John (d. 1618)   Disciplinarian who wrote in favour of episcopacy in 1587; Bp of Oxford in 1604.

Buckeridge, John (d. 1631)   Arminian; tutor to Laud; became Bp of Ely in 1608.

Burton, Henry (1578–1648)   Puritan divine. Clerk of Closet to Prince Henry and subsequently Prince Charles. Lost favour *c.* 1625. Attack on

121

bishops led to conviction and punishment by Star Chamber, 1636, along with Bastwick and Prynne.

Carleton, George (1559–1628)   Calvinist sent to Synod of Dort; Bp of Chichester in 1619.

Carr, Robert, Earl of Somerset (d. 1645)   Royal favourite until he fell from favour in 1615, partly as a result of marriage to infamous Lady Frances Howard, former wife of Earl of Essex.

Carrier, Benjamin (1566–1614)   Royal chaplain who converted to Rome in 1613.

Cartwright, Thomas (1535–1603)   Prominent Calvinist; wanted Presbyterianism in England.

Cecil, Robert (1563–1612)   Son of William Cecil; prominent Jacobean statesman; Earl of Salisbury 1605.

Cecil, William (1520– 98)   Elizabethan statesman; created Lord Burghley 1571, Lord Treasurer 1572.

Clark, Samuel (1599–1683)   Calvinist clergyman and writer of lives of eminent divines.

Clayton, Richard (d. 1612)   Early Arminian?, theologian, academic; Master of St John's College, Cambridge, in 1595; Dean of Peterborough in 1607.

Corro, Anthony (1527–91)   Spanish theologian who expressed doubts about predestination in Oxford in 1580s.

Cosin, John (1594–1672)   Arminian; chaplain to Richard Neile in 1620s; author of *Hours of Prayer,* Bp of Durham in 1660.

Cowell, John (1554–1611)   Regius Professor of Civil Law at Cambridge in 1598; author of *The Interpreter* in 1607; Vicar General to Abp of Canterbury in 1608.

Craddock, John (1573–1627)   Clergyman who became Chancellor of Durham diocese in 1619. Charged with corrupt practices in 1621 Parliament.

Curle, Walter (1575–1647)   Arminian; Bp of Winchester in 1632.

Davenant, John (1572–1641)   Lady Margaret Professor of Divinity at Cambridge 1609– 21, then became Bp of Salisbury.

De Dominis, Antonio (1566–1624)   Bp of Spalato; notable convert to Church of England in 1616; relapsed 1622.

Duck, Sir Arthur (1580–1648)   Civil lawyer; Chancellor of Bath & Wells 1616–23; Chancellor of London 1627–37; sat on High Commission 1633–41 and defended the Court before the Long Parliament.

Easdall, William (d. 1643)   Civil lawyer who rose on the staff of Richard Neile from Secretary to Chancellor of York diocese in the 1630s.

Field, John (d. 1588)   Puritan organiser active in campaigns with Cartwright and Wilcox; co-author of *An Admonition to Parliament,* 1572.

Foxe, John (1517–87)   Protestant martyrologist; author of famous *Acts and Monuments of the Church,* popularly known as *The Book of Martyrs,* first published in 1563.

Fuller, Thomas (1608–61)   Moderate Calvinist divine and Church historian; author of famous *Worthies of England,* 1662.

Goodman, Godfrey (1583–1656)   Secret Catholic who was Bp of Gloucester in 1625; reprimanded by Parliament for a sermon on the 'real presence' in 1626.

Grindal, Edmund (1519–83)   Abp of Canterbury 1575; suspended 1576.

Hall, Joseph (1574–1656)   Moderate Calvinist; Bp of Exeter in 1627; Bp of Norwich in 1641; wrote various religious works and book on episcopacy.

Hammond, Henry (1605–60)   Chaplain to Charles I; scholar and moderate divine.

Harsnett, Samuel (1561–1631)   Outspoken Arminian; caused stir as Bp of Norwich after 1619; became Abp of York in 1629.

Heylyn, Peter (1599–1662)   Laud's chaplain, religious controversialist and historian; author of *Cyprianus Anglicus.*

Hooker, Richard (1553–1600)   Author of *Laws of Ecclesiastical Polity*, published 1590s onwards.

Howard, Henry (1540–1614)   Son of Earl of Surrey who was executed in 1547. Despite Catholic inclinations he was restored to favour by James I who appointed him Lord Privy Seal.

Howard, Thomas (1561–1626)   1st Earl of Suffolk, 1603; Lord Chamberlain, 1603; Lord High Treasurer, 1614–18 before he fell from favour.

Howson, John (*c.* 1557–1632)   Arminian; Bp of Durham in 1628.

Hyde, Edward (1609–74)   Adviser to Charles I in 1640s; as Earl of Clarendon, headed Charles II's administration after Restoration; forced into exile in 1667, during which he wrote influential *History of the Rebellion.*

Jackson, Thomas (1579–1640)   Arminian; member of Durham House group; author; Bp of Peterborough in 1639.

Jewel, John (1522–71)   Bp of Salisbury and author of *Apologia*, 1562, famous defence of Church of England.

Juxon, William (1582–1663)   Friend of Laud; President of St John's College, Oxford, 1621–33; Bp of Durham, 1633; Lord Teasurer, 1636; Abp of Canterbury, 1660.

Lambe, Sir John (*c.* 1566–1646)   Civil lawyer; served as Chancellor of Peterborough, 1615; worked also in Lincoln diocese; Master of Chancery, 1622; Dean of Court of Arches, 1633.

Laud, William (1573–1645)   Arminian Abp of Canterbury in 1633; beheaded, 1645.

Leighton, Alexander (1568–1649)   Scottish physician and divine who wrote tracts against bishops, like *Sion's Plea against the Prelacie*, 1628, for which he was punished.

Lindsell, Augustine (d. 1634)   Arminian; member of Durham House group; Greek scholar; Bp of Hereford in 1633.

Mawe, Leonard (d. 1629)   Arminian; chaplain to Prince Charles in Spain; Bp of Bath & Wells in 1628.

Manwaring, Roger (1590–1653)   Cleric who preached in favour of forced loan in 1627, condemned in Parliament; Bp of St David's in 1635.

Marprelate, Martin Fictitious name adopted by author of *Martin Marprelate* tracts which lampooned bishops and state of Church in 1580s.

Montagu, James (*c.* 1568–1618) Calvinist favourite of James, whose works he edited in 1616; Bp of Winchester in 1616.

Montagu, Richard (1577–1641) Controversial Arminian theologian; wrote *A New Gagg*, 1624, and *Appello Caesarem*, 1625. Royal chaplain 1625; Bp of Chichester, 1628; Bp of Norwich, 1638.

Morton, Thomas (1564–1659) Moderate Calvinist, attended York House Conference, 1626; Bp of Durham in 1632.

Neile, Richard (1562–1640) Arminian; patron of Laud; Bp of Durham, 1617–28; Abp of York, 1632.

Overall, John (1560–1619) Arminian scholar and theologian, Regius Professor of Theology at Cambridge, 1596–1607; Bp of Norwich in 1618.

Parker, Matthew (1504–75) Calvinist; Elizabeth's first Abp of Canterbury, 1559.

Piers, John (*c.* 1523–94) Disciplinarian; colleague of Whitgift; Abp of York, 1589.

Piers, William (1580–1670) Arminian; Bp of Bath & Wells, 1632.

Potter, Barnabas (1577–1642) Moderate Calvinist; Bp of Carlisle, 1629.

Preston, John (1587–1628) Calvinist divine; preacher at Lincoln's Inn; Master of Emmanuel College, Cambridge, 1622–28; spoke at York House Conference, 1626.

Prynne, William (1600–69) Lawyer and Puritan pamphleteer; wrote anti-Arminian tracts; *Histriomastix* angered Queen in 1632; pilloried in 1634 and 1637.

Pym, John (1584–1643) Parliamentary statesman; emerged as effective leader of House of Commons in 1640; key figure in early years of Long Parliament.

Saravia, Adrian (1531–1613) French divine who came to England.

Sibthorp, Robert (d. 1662) Arminian, preached in favour of forced loan in 1627; made a royal chaplain.

Smart, Peter (1569–*c.*1652) Calvinist; prebendary of Durham who preached against Arminians in 1628 and was imprisoned; gave evidence at Laud's trial.

Travers, Walter (*c.* 1548–1635) Puritan/Presbyterian divine; friend of Beza and Cartwright.

Ussher, James (1581–1656) Moderate Calvinist theologian and scholar; Abp of Armagh, 1625.

Vorstius, Conrad (1569–1622) Dutch theologian of Remonstrant/Arminian party; took over at Leyden University on death of Arminius in 1609, but forced out of office.

Villiers, George (1592–1628) Royal favourite who became first Duke of Buckingham in 1623; assassinated in 1628.

Wentworth, Sir Thomas (1593–1641) MP and critic of royal policies; prominent advocate of Petition of Right. Lord Deputy of Ireland in

1632; subsequently created Earl of Strafford and recalled to England by Charles I in 1640. Much feared by Parliament; executed under Act of Attainder in 1641.

Whitaker, William (1548–95) Calvinist divine and academic; Regius Professor of Divinity, Cambridge, 1580; Master of St John's College, Cambridge, 1586.

White, Francis (*c.* 1564–1638) Arminian, member of Durham House group; Bp of Carlisle in 1626; Bp of Ely in 1631.

Whitgift, John (*c.* 1530–1604) Calvinist; disciplinarian; Abp of Canterbury in 1583.

Wilcox, Thomas (*c.* 1549–1608) Puritan, co-author of *Admonition to Parliament*, 1572; deprived of ministry.

Williams, John (1582–1656) Moderate Calvinist; Bp of Lincoln and Lord Keeper, 1621. Opponent of Laud, fell from favour *c.* 1625 and dismissed from Lord Keepership. Suspended from episcopal duties in 1637, but appointed Abp of York in the different political climate of 1641.

Winwood, Sir Ralph (*c.* 1563–1617) Diplomat and Secretary of State; Calvinist ally of Abbot.

Wood, Thomas (d. 1577) Puritan/Presbyterian divine; associate of Wilcox and Field.

Wren, Matthew (1585–1667) Arminian divine; royal chaplain; Clerk of Closet in 1633; Dean of Chapel Royal, 1636; Bp of Ely, 1638.

Bibliography

PRIMARY SOURCES

1   Anon, *Episcopall Inheritance*, Oxford, 1641.
2   *A Petition presented to the Parliament from the County of Nottingham*, 1641.
3   Bettenson, H. (ed.), *Documents of the Christian Church*, Oxford University Press, 2nd edition, 1967.
4   Birch, T. (ed.), *The Court and Times of Charles I*, 2 vols, 1848.
5   *Calendar State Papers Domestic, Charles I 1635*, ed. J. Bruce, 1865.
6   Cardwell, E. (ed.), *Documentary Annals of the Reformed Church of England*, 2 vols, Oxford University Press, 1844 edition.
7   Cardwell, E. (ed.), *Synodalia*, 2 vols, Oxford University Press, 1842.
8   *Certain Sermons or Homilies appointed to be read in Churches*, Oxford University Press, 1840 edition.
9   Chandos, J. (ed.), *In God's Name, Examples of Preaching in England 1534–1662*, Hutchinson, 1971.
10   Collinson P., 'Letters of Thomas Wood, Puritan, 1566–1577' in *Godly People, Essays on English Protestantism and Puritanism*, ed. P. Collinson, Hambledon Press, 1983.
11   Cross, M. C. (ed.), *The Royal Supremacy in the Elizabethan Church*, Allen & Unwin, 1969.
12   Elton, G. R. (ed.), *The Tudor Constitution*, Cambridge University Press, 2nd edition, 1982.
13   Fell, J., *The Life of the Reverend Henry Hammond*, Oxford University Press, 1806 edition.
14   Foster, E. R. (ed.), *Proceedings in Parliament 1610*, 2 vols, Yale University Press, 1966.
15   Fuller, T., *The Holy State*, 3rd edition, 1652.
16   Fuller, T., *The Church History of Britain*, 1842 edition.
17   Fuller, T., *Pulpit Sparks*, ed. Rev. M. Fuller, 1886.
18   Gardiner, S. R. (ed.), *The Constitutional Documents of the Puritan Revolution 1625–1660*, Oxford University Press, 3rd revised edition, 1906.
19   Groos, G. W. (trans. and ed.), *The Diary of Baron Waldstein*, Thames & Hudson, 1981.
20   Hall, J., *The Shaking of the Olive Tree*, 1660.
21   Heylyn, P. *Cyprianus Anglicus*, 1668.
22   *Historical MSS Commission, Eleventh Report*, Appendix, Part 1, 1887.

23 Hutchinson, F. (ed.), *The Works of George Herbert*, Oxford University Press, 1941.
24 Hutchinson, L., *Memoirs of the Life of Colonel Hutchinson*, Everyman edition, 1968.
25 Johnstone, H. (ed.), *Churchwardens' Presentments (17th Century), Part 1 Archdeaconry of Chichester*, Sussex Record Society, XLIX, 1948.
26 Joyce, J. (ed.), *A Constitutional History of the Convocation of the Clergy*, 1855, Gregg Press Reprint, 1967.
27 Kenyon, J. (ed.), *The Stuart Constitution*, Cambridge University Press, 2nd edition, 1986.
28 Laud, W., *Works*, ed. J. Bliss and W. Scott, 7 vols, Oxford, 1847–60.
29 More, P. and Cross, F. (eds), *Anglicanism*, SPCK, 1962.
30 Notestein, W. (ed.), *Journal of Sir Symonds D'Ewes*, Oxford University Press, 1923.
31 Notestein, W. and Relf, F. (eds), *Commons Debates for 1629*, Minnesota University Press, 1921.
32 Prynne, W., *The Antipathie of the English Lordly Prelacie*, 1641.
33 Prynne, W., *A Looking Glass for all Lordly Prelates*, 1636.
34 Rushworth, J. (ed.), *Historical Collections*, 8 vols, 1721 edition.
35 Selden, J., *Table-Talk*, 1696 edition.
36 Stirry, T., *A Rot amongst the Bishops or a Terrible Tempest in the Sea of Canterbury*, 1641.
37 Sutcliffe, M., *A Treatise of Ecclesiasticall Discipline*, 1590.
38 Tanner, J. R. (ed.), *Constitutional Documents of the Reign of James I 1603–1625*, Cambridge University Press, 1952 edition.

SECONDARY SOURCES

Books
39 Acheson, R. J., *Radical Puritans in England 1550–1660*, Longman, 1990.
40 Aveling, J. C. H., *The Handle and the Axe. The Catholic Recusants in England from Reformation to Emancipation*, Blond & Briggs, 1976.
41 Bossy, J., *The English Catholic Community 1570–1850*, Darton, Longman & Todd, 1975.
42 Carlton, C., *Charles I*, Routledge & Kegan Paul, 1983.
43 Carlton, C., *Archbishop William Laud*, Routledge & Kegan Paul, 1987.
44 Cliffe, J. T., *The Puritan Gentry*, Routledge, 1984.
45 Collinson, P., *The Elizabethan Puritan Movement*, Cape, 1967.
46 Collinson, P., *Archbishop Grindal 1519–1583*, Cape, 1979.
47 Collinson, P., *The Religion of Protestants*, Oxford University Press, 1982.
48 Collinson, P., *English Puritanism*, Historical Association, 1983.
49 Collinson, P., *The Birthpangs of Protestant England*, Macmillan, 1988.
50 Cope, E. S., *Politics Without Parliament 1629–1640*, Allen & Unwin, 1987.

51 Coward, B., *Social Change and Continuity in Early Modern England 1550–1750*, Longman, 1988.

52 Cross, M. C., *Church and People*, Fontana, 1976.

53 Cust, R. and Hughes, A. (eds), *Conflict in Early Stuart England: Studies in Religion and Politics 1603–1642*, Longman, 1989.

54 Davies, J., *The Caroline Captivity of the Church*, Oxford University Press, 1992.

55 Doran, S. and Durston, C., *Princes, Pastors and People: The Church and Religion in England 1529–1689*, Routledge, 1991.

56 Dures, A., *English Catholicism 1558–1642*, Longman, 1983.

57 Eales, J., *Puritans and Roundheads: The Harleys of Brampton Bryan and the Outbreak of the English Civil War*, Cambridge University Press, 1990.

58 Fincham, K., *Prelate as Pastor: The Episcopate of James I*, Oxford University Press, 1990.

59 Fletcher, A., *A County Community in Peace and War: Sussex 1600–1660*, Longman, 1975.

60 Graves, M., *The Tudor Parliaments, Crown, Lords and Commons 1485–1603*, Longman, 1985.

61 Haigh, C. (ed.), *The Reign of Elizabeth I*, Macmillan, 1984.

62 Haller, W., *Foxe's Book of Martyrs and the Elect Nation*, Cape, 1963.

63 Haugaard, W., *Elizabeth and the English Reformation*, Cambridge University Press, 1968.

64 Heal, F. M. and O'Day, R. (eds), *Church and Society in England: Henry VIII to James I*, Macmillan, 1977.

65 Heal, F. M. and O'Day, R. (eds), *Princes and Paupers in the English Church 1500–1800*, Leicester University Press, 1981.

66 Heal, F. M., *Of Prelates and Princes: A Study of the Economic and Social Position of the Tudor Episcopate*, Cambridge University Press, 1980.

67 Hibbard, C., *Charles I and the Popish Plot*, North Carolina University Press, 1983.

68 Higham, F., *Catholic and Reformed: A Study of the Anglican Church 1559–1662*, SPCK, 1962.

69 Hill, C., *The English Revolution 1640*, Lawrence & Wishart, 1940.

70 Hill, C., *Economic Problems of the Church from Archbishop Whitgift to the Long Parliament*, Oxford University Press, 1956.

71 Hill, C., *Society and Puritanism in Pre-revolutionary England*, Secker & Warburg, 1964.

72 Hill, C., *Antichrist in Seventeenth Century England*, Oxford University Press, 1971.

73 Hill, C., *Change and Continuity in Seventeenth Century England*, Weidenfeld & Nicolson, 1974.

74 Hill, C., *A Nation of Change and Novelty*, Routledge, 1990.

75 Hirst, D., *Authority and Conflict: England 1603–1658*, Edward Arnold, 1986.

76 Houlbrooke, R., *Church Courts and People during the English Reformation 1520–1570*, Oxford University Press, 1979.

77 Hughes, A., *The Causes of the English Civil War*, Macmillan, 1991.

78 Hunt, W., *The Puritan Moment: The Coming of Revolution in an English County*, Harvard University Press, 1983.

79 Ingram, M., *Church Courts, Sex and Marriage in England, 1570–1640*, Cambridge University Press, 1987.

80 Jones, N. L., *Faith by Statute: Parliament and the Settlement of Religion 1559*, Royal Historical Society, 1982.

81 Kearney, H., *Scholars and Gentlemen: Universities and Society in Pre-industrial Britain*, Faber & Faber, 1970.

82 Kendall, R., *Calvin and English Calvinism to 1649*, Oxford University Press, 1979.

83 Lake, P., *Moderate Puritans and the Elizabethan Church*, Cambridge University Press, 1982.

84 Lake, P., *Anglicans and Puritans? Presbyterianism and English Conformist Thought from Whitgift to Hooker*, Unwin Hyman, 1988.

85 Lake, P. and Dowling, M. (eds), *Protestantism and the National Church in Sixteenth Century England*, Croom Helm, 1987.

86 Laslett, P., *The World we have Lost*, Methuen, 2nd edition, 1971.

87 Levack, B., *The Civil Lawyers of England*, Oxford University Press, 1973.

88 Lockyer, R., *The Early Stuarts: A Political History of England 1603–1642*, Longman, 1989.

89 Lockyer, R., *Buckingham: The Life and Political Career of George Villiers, First Duke of Buckingham 1592–1628*, Longman 1981.

90 Macaulay, T. B., *The History of England*, 3 vols, Everyman edition, 1906.

91 MacCulloch, D., *The Later Reformation in England 1547–1603*, Macmillan, 1990.

92 MacFarlane, A., *Witchcraft in Tudor and Stuart England*, Routledge & Kegan Paul, 1970.

93 Marchant, R., *The Puritans and the Church Courts in the Diocese of York 1560–1642*, Longman, 1960.

94 Marchant, R., *The Church under the Law: Justice, Administration and Discipline in the Diocese of York 1569–1640*, Cambridge University Press, 1969.

95 Marcombe, D. (ed.), *The Last Principality. Politics, Religion and Society in the Bishopric of Durham, 1494–1660*, Nottingham University Press, 1987.

96 Morgan, I., *Prince Charles's Puritan Chaplain*, George Allen & Unwin, 1957.

97 Morrill, J. (ed.), *Reactions to the English Civil War 1642–1649*, Macmillan, 1982.

98 New, J., *Anglican and Puritan*, Stanford University Press, 1964.

99 O'Day, R. and Heal, F. M. (eds), *Continuity and Change: Personnel and Administration of the Church of England 1500–1642*, Leicester University Press, 1976.

Bibliography

100 O'Day, R., *The English Clergy: The Emergence and Consolidation of a Profession 1558–1642*, Leicester University Press, 1979.

101 Porter, H. C., *Reformation and Reaction in Tudor Cambridge*, Cambridge University Press, 1958.

102 Phythian-Adams, C., *Local History and Folklore: A new Framework*, Bedford Square Press, 1975.

103 Richardson, R. C., *Puritanism in North-west England: A Regional Study of the Diocese of Chester to 1642*, Manchester University Press, 1972.

104 Russell, C., *Parliaments and English Politics 1621–1629*, Oxford University Press, 1979.

105 Russell, C., *The Causes of the English Civil War*, Oxford University Press, 1990.

106 Seaver, P., *The Puritan Lectureships*, Stanford University Press, 1970.

107 Seaver, P., *Wallington's World: A Puritan Artisan in Seventeenth Century London*, Methuen, 1985.

108 Sellar, W. C. and Yeatman, R. J., *1066 And All That*, Penguin edition, 1960.

109 Sharpe, J., *Defamation and Sexual Slander in Early Modern England: The Church Courts at York*, Borthwick Papers, 58, 1980.

110 Sharpe, K., *The Personal Rule of Charles I*, Yale University Press, 1992.

111 Sheils, W. J., *The Puritans in the Diocese of Peterborough 1570–1610*, Northants. Record Society, 1979.

112 Sheils, W. J., *The English Reformation 1530–1570*, Longman, 1991.

113 Solt, L., *Church and State in Early Modern England 1509–1640*, Oxford University Press, 1990.

114 Sommerville, J., *Politics and Ideology in England 1603–1640*, Longman, 1986.

115 Thomas, K., *Religion and the Decline of Magic*, Penguin edition, 1973.

116 Trevor-Roper, H., *Archbishop Laud 1573–1645*, Macmillan, 2nd edition, 1962.

117 Trevor-Roper, H., *Catholics, Anglicans and Puritans: Seventeenth Century Essays*, Secker & Warburg, 1987.

118 Tyacke, N., *Anti-Calvinists: The Rise of English Arminianism c. 1590–1640*, Oxford University Press, 1987.

119 Tyacke, N., *The Fortunes of English Puritanism 1603–1640*, Friends of Dr Williams's Library, 1990.

120 Underdown, D., *Revel, Riot and Rebellion: Popular Politics and Culture in England 1603–1660*, Oxford University Press, 1985.

121 Usher, R., *The Rise and Fall of the High Commission*, Oxford University Press reprint, 1968.

122 Usher, R., *The Reconstruction of the English Church*, 2 vols, Gregg International Publishers reprint, 1969.

123 Walzer, M., *The Revolution of the Saints*, Harvard University Press, 1965.

124 Welsby, P., *George Abbot, the Unwanted Archbishop 1562–1633*, SPCK, 1962.

125 Welsby, P., *Lancelot Andrewes 1555–1626*, SPCK, 1958.
126 White, P., *Predestination, Policy and Polemic*, Cambridge University Press, 1992.
127 Wrightson, K. and Levine, D., *Poverty and Piety in an English Village: Terling 1525–1700*, Academic Press, 1979.

Articles and essays
Abbreviations: *EHR*   *English Historical Review*
                 HJ   *Historical Journal*
                 HR   *Historical Research*
                 JBS   *Journal of British Studies*
                 JEH   *Journal of Ecclesiastical History*
                 P&P   *Past and Present*
                 SCH   *Studies in Church History*
                 TRHS   *Transactions of the Royal Historical Society*

128 Bernard, G., 'The Church of England *c.* 1529– *c.* 1642', *History*, 75 (244), 1990.
129 Bossy, J., 'The English Catholic community 1603–1625', in *The Reign of James VI and I*, ed. A. G. Smith, Macmillan, 1973.
130 Calder, J., 'A seventeenth century attempt to purify the Anglican Church', [The Feoffees for Impropriations], *American Historical Review*, 53, 1948.
131 Christianson, P., 'From expectation to militance: reformers and Babylon in the first two years of the Long Parliament', *JEH*, XXIV (3), 1973.
132 Clifton, R., 'Fear of Popery', in *The Origins of the English Civil War*, ed. C. Russell, Macmillan, 1975.
133 Collinson, P., 'Shepherds, sheepdogs, and hirelings: the pastoral ministry in post-Reformation England', *SCH*, 26, 1989.
134 Collinson, P., 'The Elizabethan Church and the new religion', in *The Reign of Elizabeth I*, ed. C. Haigh, Macmillan, 1984.
135 Collinson, P., 'The Jacobean religious settlement: the Hampton Court Conference', in *Before the English Civil War*, ed. H. Tomlinson, Macmillan, 1983.
136 Cope, E., 'The bishops and parliamentary politics in early Stuart England', *Parliamentary History*, 9(1), 1990.
137 Croft, P., 'The religion of Robert Cecil', *HJ*, 34(4), 1991.
138 Cross, C., 'Dens of loitering lubbers: Protestant protest against cathedral foundations, 1540–1640', *SCH*, 9, 1972.
139 Curtis, M., 'The Hampton Court Conference and its aftermath', *History*, 46, 1961.
140 Cust, R., 'Anti-Puritanism and Urban Politics: Charles I and Great Yarmouth', *HJ*, 35(1), 1992.
141 Davies, G., 'Arminian versus Puritan in England, ca. 1620–1640', *Huntington Library Bulletin*, 5, 1934.

142 Donegan, B., 'The York House Conference revisited: laymen, Calvinism and Arminianism', *HR*, 64(155), 1991.

143 Fielding, J., 'Opposition to the personal rule of Charles I: the diary of Robert Woodford, 1637–1641', *HJ*, 31(4), 1988.

144 Fincham, K., 'Ramifications of the Hampton Court Conference in the dioceses 1603–1609', *JEH*, 36(2), 1985.

145 Fincham, K., 'Prelacy and politics: Archbishop Abbot's defence of Protestant orthodoxy', *HR*, 61, 1988.

146 Fincham, K. and Lake, P., 'The ecclesiastical policy of King James I', *JBS*, 24, 1985.

147 Fletcher, A., 'Concern for renewal in the Root and Branch debates of 1641', *SCH*, 14, 1977.

148 Foster, A. W., 'The function of a bishop: the career of Richard Neile, 1562–1640', in *Continuity and Change*, ed. R. O'Day and F. Heal, Leicester University Press, 1976.

149 Foster, A. W., 'Chichester diocese in the early seventeenth century', *Sussex Archaeological Collections*, 123, 1985.

150 Foster, A. W., 'Church policies of the 1630s', in *Conflict in Early Stuart England: Studies in Religion and Politics 1600–1642*, ed. R. Cust and A. Hughes, Longman, 1989.

151 George, C., 'Puritanism as history and historiography', *P&P*, 41, 1968.

152 Grayson, C., 'James I and the religious crisis in the United Provinces 1613–1619', *SCH*, Subsidia 2, 1979.

153 Green, I., 'The persecution of "scandalous" and "malignant" parish clergy during the English Civil War', *EHR*, 94(372), 1979.

154 Green, I., 'Career prospects and clerical conformity in the early Stuart Church', *P&P*, 90, 1981.

155 Green I., '"Reformed pastors" and bons curés: the changing role of the parish clergy in early modern Europe', *SCH*, 26, 1989.

156 Haigh, C., 'From monopoly to minority: Catholicism in early modern England', *TRHS*, 5th ser., XXI, 1981.

157 Haigh, C., 'Finance and administration in a new diocese: Chester 1541–1641', in *Continuity and Change*, ed. R. O'Day and F. Heal, Leicester University Press, 1976.

158 Haigh, C., 'Puritan evangelism in the reign of Elizabeth I', *EHR*, 92(362), 1977.

159 Hall, B., 'Puritanism: the problem of definition', *SCH*, 11, 1965.

160 Hoenderdaal, G., 'The debate about Arminians outside the Netherlands', in *Leiden University in the Seventeenth Century*, ed. Th. H. Lunsingh Scheurleer and G. Posthumus Meyjes, Leyden, 1975.

161 Holland, S. M., 'George Abbot: "the wanted Archbishop"', *Church History*, 56(2), 1987.

162 Hughes, A., 'Thomas Dugard and his circle in the 1630s – a parliamentary Puritan connexion?', *HJ*, 29(4), 1986.

163 Ingram, M., 'Religion, communities and moral discipline in late sixteenth- and early seventeenth-century England: case studies', in *Religion and Society in Early Modern Europe 1500–1800*, ed. Kaspar van Greyerz, Allen & Unwin, 1984.

164 Kautz, A., 'The selection of Jacobean bishops', in *Early Stuart Studies: Essays in Honor of David Harris Willson*, ed. H. Reinmuth, Jr, Minnesota University Press, 1970.

165 Kennedy, D., 'The Jacobean episcopate', *HJ*, 5, 1962.

166 Lake, P., 'Calvinism and the English Church 1570 –1635', *P&P*, 114, 1987.

167 Lake, P., 'Conformist clericalism? Richard Bancroft's analysis of the socio-economic roots of Presbyterianism', *SCH*, 24, 1983.

168 Lambert, S., 'Committees, religion and parliamentary encroachment on royal authority in early Stuart England', *EHR*, 105(414), 1990.

169 Lambert S., 'Richard Montagu, Arminianism and censorship', *P&P*, 124, 1989.

170 Lindley, K., 'The lay Catholics of England in the reign of Charles I', *JEH*, 22, 1971.

171 MacCulloch, D., 'Arminius and the Arminians', *History Today*, Oct. 1989.

172 MacCulloch, D., 'The myth of the English Reformation', *JBS*, 30, 1991.

173 McGee, J. S., 'William Laud and the outward face of religion', in *Leaders of the Reformation*, ed. R. DeMolen, Associated University Presses, 1984.

174 McGrath, P., 'Elizabethan Catholicism: a reconsideration', *JEH*, 35(3), 1984.

175 Morrill, J., 'The attack on the Church of England in the Long Parliament 1640–1642', in *History, Society and the Churches, Essays in Honour of Owen Chadwick*, ed. D. Beales and G. Best, Cambridge University Press, 1985.

176 Morrill, J., 'The religious context of the English Civil War', *TRHS*, 5th ser., 34, 1984.

177 O'Day, R., 'Cumulative debt: the bishops of Coventry and Lichfield and their economic problems, c. 1540 –1640', *Midland History*, 3(2), 1975.

178 Parker, T., 'Arminianism and Laudianism in seventh century England', *SCH*, 1, 1964.

179 Phillips, H., 'The last years of the Court of Star Chamber, 1630–41', *TRHS*, 4th ser., 21, 1939.

180 Quintrell, B., 'The royal hunt and the Puritans, 1604–1605', *JEH*, 31(1), 1980.

181 Reay, B., 'Popular religion', in *Popular Culture in Seventeenth Century England*, ed. B. Reay, Croom Helm, 1985.

182 Rogan, J., 'King James's bishops', *Durham University Journal*, 1956.

183 Schwartz, H., 'Arminianism and the English Parliament, 1624 –1629', *JBS*, 112, 1973.

184 Sharpe, J., 'Scandalous and malignant priests in Essex: the impact of grassroots Puritanism', in *Politics and People in Revolutionary England*, ed. C. Jones, M. Newitt and S. Roberts, Blackwell, 1986.

185 Sharpe, K., 'Archbishop Laud', *History Today*, 33, Aug. 1983.

186 Sharpe, K., 'Archbishop William Laud and the University of Oxford', in *Politics and Ideas in Early Stuart England*, K. Sharpe, Pinter Publishers, 1989.

187 Shriver, F., 'Orthodoxy and diplomacy: James I and the Vorstius Affair', *EHR*, 85(336), 1970.

188 Shriver, F., 'Hampton Court re-visited: James I and the Puritans', *JEH*, 33(1), 1982.

189 Spufford, M., 'Can we count the "godly" and the "conformable" in the seventeenth century?', *JEH*, 36(3), 1985.

190 Trevor-Roper, H., 'King James and his bishops', *History Today*, Sept. 1955.

191 Tyacke, N., 'Arminianism and English culture', in *Britain and the Netherlands*, vol. VII, 'Church and state since the Reformation', ed. A. Duke and C. Tanse, The Hague; Martinus Nijhoff, 1981.

192 Tyacke, N., 'Puritanism, Arminianism and counter-revolution', in *The Origins of the English Civil War*, ed. C. Russell, Macmillan, 1973.

193 Tyacke, N. and White, P., 'Debate: Arminianism reconsidered', *P&P*, 115, 1987.

194 White, P., 'The rise of Arminianism reconsidered', *P&P*, 101, 1983.

195 Wiener, C., 'The beleagured isle, a study of Elizabethan and early Jacobean anti-Catholicism', *P&P*, 51, 1971.

Theses

196 Britton, A., 'The House of Lords in English politics 1604–1614', Unpublished Oxford D. Phil. thesis, 1982.

197 Shriver, F., 'The ecclesiastical policy of James I. Two aspects: the Puritans (1603–1605), the Arminians (1611–1625)', Unpublished Cambridge Ph.D. thesis, 1967.

Index